A 3-Day Travel Guide

via Sandra Filipe Photography

Welcome to **Lisbon,** the charming and vibrant capital of Portugal! Whether you're a first-time visitor or a seasoned traveler, Lisbon has something for everyone. With our travel guide "Lisbon in 3 days," you'll discover the best of what this amazing city has to offer in just three days.

Our guide is designed to help you make the most of your time in Lisbon. We've created a comprehensive plan that takes you through the city's highlights, from historic landmarks to trendy neighborhoods, and everything in between.

In this ebook, you'll find expert recommendations on where to stay, what to see, and where to eat. We've also included practical information on transportation, so you can easily navigate the city and get the most out of your trip. With "Lisbon in 3 days," you won't have to worry about missing out on the best sights and experiences Lisbon has to offer. Our guide takes you on a journey through the city's rich culture, history, and cuisine, giving you an unforgettable experience in just three days. So, let's get started and explore Lisbon!

Contents

Introduction

1.1. A Brief History of Lisbon

Lisbon is a city with a rich and complex history that dates back thousands of years. From its humble beginnings as a small trading post to its status as a world-renowned cultural and economic center, the story of Lisbon is one that has captivated historians and visitors alike.

Prehistoric Era

The area that is now Lisbon was first inhabited by humans during the prehistoric era, as far back as the 8th millennium BCE. The region's natural harbor made it an ideal location for trade and commerce, and it quickly became an important center for early human civilization.

Roman Era

In 205 BCE, the Romans conquered Lisbon and established a settlement in the area that is now known as the Alfama neighborhood. The city, which was known as Olissipo, quickly became an important trading center and was renowned for its wine and olive oil production.

Over the centuries, Lisbon continued to thrive under Roman rule, and the city's population grew to more than 20,000 people. The Romans built several important landmarks and buildings, including the Lisbon Cathedral and the Roman Theater, which can still be seen in the city today.

Middle Ages

Following the fall of the Roman Empire, Lisbon was conquered by the Visigoths, who ruled the city from the 5th to the 8th century. In the 8th century, the Moors conquered Lisbon, and the city became a center for Islamic culture and commerce.

During the Middle Ages, Lisbon continued to thrive, and it was known for its impressive architecture and culture. In 1147, the city was reconquered by Christian forces, and it became an important center for trade and commerce once again.

Renaissance Era

During the Renaissance, Lisbon experienced a period of great cultural and economic growth. The city was home to several prominent artists and thinkers, including Vasco da Gama, who discovered a sea route to India in 1498.

In the 16th century, Lisbon became one of the wealthiest and most powerful cities in Europe, and it was renowned for its impressive architecture and cultural achievements. The city's wealth and power continued to grow over the centuries, and it became a center for trade, commerce, and art.

Modern Era

In the 18th century, Lisbon was devastated by a massive earthquake that destroyed much of the city and killed thousands of people. Despite the destruction, the city was quickly rebuilt, and it continued to grow and prosper over the centuries.

In the 20th century, Lisbon became an important cultural and political center, and it played a key role in the Portuguese Revolution of 1974. Today, Lisbon is a vibrant and diverse city that is home to a rich and fascinating history

1.2. Language and Culture

Lisbon, the capital of Portugal, is a vibrant city known for its rich history, diverse culture, and welcoming atmosphere. As a visitor, it's important to understand the city's language and cultural nuances to make the most of your trip.

Language:

The official language of Lisbon is Portuguese. While many locals, particularly those in the tourism and hospitality sectors, speak English, it's always appreciated when visitors attempt to learn some basic Portuguese phrases. Key phrases include "Bom dia" (Good morning), "Por favor" (Please), "Obrigado/Obrigada" (Thank you, for males/females, respectively), and "Desculpe" (Excuse me/I'm sorry). Spanish, French, and German are also commonly spoken among the locals.

Culture:

Portuguese culture is a fascinating blend of various influences, owing to the country's rich history and its connection with numerous global empires. Lisbon, in particular, has been shaped by Roman, Visigoth, and Moorish settlements, as well as the Age of Discoveries, when Portugal led maritime expeditions around the world.

Fado: One of the most important aspects of Lisbon's culture is Fado, a traditional Portuguese music genre characterized by mournful tunes and lyrics. To truly experience Lisbon's soul, consider attending a Fado performance in a local "casa de fado" or Fado house.

Azulejos: Lisbon is famous for its beautiful, hand-painted ceramic tiles called Azulejos. These decorative tiles adorn numerous buildings, churches, and palaces throughout the city, reflecting its rich history and artistic heritage.

Gastronomy: Portuguese cuisine is another significant aspect of Lisbon's culture. Expect to find a variety of seafood dishes, hearty meat stews, and delicious pastries during your stay. Don't forget to try the iconic "Pastel de Nata," a scrumptious custard tart, and "Bacalhau," the nation's beloved salted cod.

Laid-back lifestyle: The Portuguese people are known for their warm and welcoming nature, as well as their relaxed and easygoing lifestyle. Lisbonites often socialize at cafés, bars, and esplanades, enjoying the city's pleasant climate and beautiful views. Embrace the slower pace and allow yourself to unwind and enjoy the city's charm.

Traditions and Festivals: Lisbon hosts a variety of traditional festivals and events throughout the year, such as "Santos Populares" (Popular Saints), which take place in June. These festivities feature parades, street parties, and lively music, providing an excellent opportunity to immerse yourself in the local culture.

Lunchtime in Portugal is approximately between 1 p.m. and 3 p.m. **Dinnertime** starts at around 9 p.m. and goes until 11 p.m. Just as a comparison, Portugal's neighbors – the Spanish – have their meals way later. Despite this, both Portuguese and Spanish natives share as a common trait the habit of staying in the table for a long while to talk and thoroughly enjoy their meal and mutual company. It is definitely part of the culture to connect over food and drinks and to prolong it for longer than it should take to eat your meal, becoming a genuinely memorable bonding experience.

Moreover, the Portuguese have long maintained a habit of drinking a shot of expresso in the morning, after lunch and after dinner. **«Café» and «Bica»** are the names most commonly used to ask for an expresso. So, if you want to adventure and take this shot of caffeine, just say «Era uma bica, se faz favor! ».

In Portugal, the legal drinking age is 18. Furthermore, it is possible to drink alcohol on the streets and to carry bottles with you without breaking any law.

It also may be useful to know that in Portugal **tipping** is not mandatory and definitely not included in the receipt and final cost of the meal. It is a rather common practice to leave something after you pay, usually 2 or 3 euros, but rarely does anyone give more than that. Furthermore, no one will look at you differently or think it's strange if you don't leave a tip.

Another common practice in Portugal has to do with how you talk to older people, people you don't know or are not particularly familiar with. Formally, and as a demonstration of respect, people use «você.» But there is a little twist. It is considered rude in Portugal to actually use the word «você,» so it is omitted. The sentence stays the same, the verb is conjugated in the 3rd person singular, but «você» is either omitted or replaced by the person's name or just «o senhor / a senhora» (sir / ma'am). Look at these examples:

Did you eat the cookies, sir? – (O senhor) *Comeu* as bolachas?

You're an incredible mother! – (A senhora) *É* uma mãe incrível!

Filipa, do you want to come by for dinner? – (A Filipa) *Quer* vir cá jantar?

Perceiving these differences as a foreign speaker may be hard. Do not worry, though, if you end up saying "tu" instead of either omitting or saying "você" – everyone will understand that you are foreign trying hard to speak their beautiful language, and most certainly won't take it the wrong way, on the contrary – they will appreciate your effort and consideration.

1.4. Climate and Best Time to Visit

Lisbon, situated along Portugal's western coast, boasts a Mediterranean climate characterized by mild, wet winters and warm, sunny summers. Understanding the city's climate and determining the best time to visit will ensure you can make the most of your trip to this beautiful destination.

Climate: Lisbon enjoys a pleasant climate year-round, with an average annual temperature of 17°C (63°F). The city experiences around 2,800 hours of sunshine per year, making it one of the sunniest capitals in Europe.

Winter (December to February): Lisbon's winters are relatively mild, with average temperatures ranging between 8°C (46°F) and 15°C (59°F). Rain is more common during these months, although it's still possible to enjoy some sunny days. This is also the low season for tourism, making it a good time to visit if you prefer fewer crowds and lower accommodation prices.

Spring (March to May): Spring is a delightful time to visit Lisbon, as temperatures begin to rise and the city's flora comes alive. Average temperatures range from 12°C (54°F) in March to 18°C (64°F) in May. Rainfall decreases during this period, and the number of sunny days increases, providing ideal conditions for sightseeing.

Summer (June to August): Summers in Lisbon are warm and sunny, with average temperatures ranging from 21°C (70°F) to 28°C (82°F), and occasional heatwaves pushing temperatures above 30°C (86°F). This is peak tourist season, so expect larger crowds and higher accommodation prices. It's a great time to enjoy Lisbon's beaches, outdoor events, and vibrant nightlife.

Autumn (September to November): Autumn in Lisbon is characterized by mild temperatures and gradually increasing rainfall. September remains warm, with average temperatures around 23°C (73°F), while November sees cooler temperatures averaging 15°C (59°F). This is a pleasant time to visit, as the city is less crowded than during the summer months, and the changing foliage adds to Lisbon's charm.

Best Time to Visit: The best time to visit Lisbon depends on your preferences and interests. Spring (March to May) and autumn (September to November) are considered the most favorable times to visit, as the weather is pleasant and the city is less crowded than during the summer months. These seasons also offer a better chance of finding reasonable accommodation rates.

Summer is the ideal time for beachgoers, outdoor enthusiasts, and those looking to experience Lisbon's lively events and festivals. However, keep in mind that the city will be more crowded and prices for accommodations will be higher.

If you're on a budget and don't mind cooler temperatures and occasional rain, winter can be a great time to explore Lisbon without the crowds. Just be prepared for shorter daylight hours and some attractions operating on limited hours or closed for maintenance.

Ultimately, Lisbon is a captivating destination regardless of the time of year, and each season offers its unique charm and experiences.

1.5. Getting to Lisbon

Lisbon, as a major European capital, is well-connected by air, land, and sea. The following are the most common ways to reach the city, along with helpful websites and general price ranges for each mode of transportation:

By Air:

Lisbon is served by **Humberto Delgado Airport (LIS),** also known as **Lisbon Portela Airport,** located about 7 kilometers (4.3 miles) north of the city center. The airport is a hub for the country's flag carrier, TAP Air Portugal, and welcomes numerous international flights from Europe, North America, South America, Africa, and Asia.

Websites to check for flights:

- Skyscanner (https://www.skyscanner.com/)

- Google Flights (https://www.google.com/flights/)

- Kayak (https://www.kayak.com/flights)

Prices: Flight prices vary depending on your departure city, the time of year, and how far in advance you book. For example, a round-trip economy flight from New York City to Lisbon might cost between $400 and $800, while a flight from London could range from $60 to $200.

By Train:

Lisbon has excellent rail connections with other cities in Portugal and major European destinations. The city's primary train stations are Santa Apolónia and Oriente, both of which serve domestic and international routes.

Websites to check train tickets:

- Comboios de Portugal (CP) for domestic routes (https://www.cp.pt/)

- Renfe for trains from Spain (https://www.renfe.com/)

- Eurail for European rail passes (https://www.eurail.com/)

Prices: Train ticket prices vary based on the type of train, the distance traveled, and the class of service. A one-way train ticket from Porto to Lisbon might cost between €25 and €50, while a ticket from Madrid could range from €50 to €150.

By Bus:

Long-distance buses, or "**autocarros**," connect Lisbon with other cities in Portugal and major destinations across Europe. The main bus terminal in Lisbon is Sete Rios, which is conveniently connected to the city's metro system.

Websites to check for bus tickets:

- Rede Expressos for domestic routes (https://www.rede-expressos.pt/)

- FlixBus for international routes (https://www.flixbus.com/)

- Eurolines for European bus routes (https://www.eurolines.eu/)

Prices: Bus fares are generally more affordable than train fares, although travel times may be longer. A one-way bus ticket from Porto to Lisbon could cost between €15 and €30, while a ticket from Madrid might range from €40 to €70.

By Car:

Lisbon can be easily accessed by car via a network of well-maintained highways, such as the A1 from Porto or the A2 from the Algarve region. Keep in mind that tolls apply on most Portuguese highways. If you're driving from another European country, make sure to comply with each nation's specific road rules and regulations.

Websites for car rental and route planning:

- AutoEurope (https://www.autoeurope.com/)

- Rentalcars (https://www.rentalcars.com/)

- ViaMichelin for route planning (https://www.viamichelin.com/)

Prices: Car rental prices vary depending on the type of vehicle, rental duration, and pick-up location. A compact car rental for a week in Lisbon could cost between €150 and €300, not including fuel and tolls.

Please note that the prices provided are for reference only and are subject to change based on various factors.

1.6. Travel Tips and Safety

Lisbon is generally a safe and welcoming city for visitors. However, it's essential to be aware of your surroundings and take necessary precautions to ensure a smooth and enjoyable trip. Here are some specific travel tips and safety advice for visiting Lisbon:

1. **Pickpocketing and Petty Theft:** Like any major city, Lisbon has its share of pickpockets, especially in crowded tourist areas and on public transportation. Keep your belongings secure and be mindful of your surroundings. Avoid displaying expensive items or large amounts of cash, and consider using a money belt or neck pouch to store your passport and valuables.

2. **Navigating Lisbon's Hills and Cobblestones:** Lisbon is known for its steep hills and narrow, cobblestone streets. Wear comfortable, non-slip shoes to navigate the city safely, and be cautious in wet conditions, as the cobblestones can become slippery.

3. **Public Transportation Etiquette:** When using Lisbon's metro, buses, or trams, be sure to validate your ticket upon boarding to avoid fines. The historic Tram 28 is a popular tourist attraction but can be crowded and a target for pickpockets. Consider riding the tram early in the morning or later in the evening to avoid peak times.

4. **Taxis and Ridesharing:** While taxis are generally safe and reliable in Lisbon, it's important to ensure the taxi is licensed, with a visible meter and identification. Alternatively, use ridesharing apps like Uber, Bolt, or Kapten for added convenience and safety.

5. **Driving in Lisbon:** If you choose to drive in Lisbon, be aware that the city's narrow, winding streets and heavy traffic can be challenging for inexperienced drivers. Parking is also limited and can be expensive in the city center. Familiarize yourself with local traffic rules, and pay attention to tram lines and pedestrian areas.

6. **Ocean Safety:** When visiting Lisbon's beaches, be cautious of strong currents and riptides, especially on the western coast. Always swim in designated swimming areas and heed the advice of local lifeguards.

7. **Emergency Contacts:** In case of an emergency, dial 112 for police, ambulance, or fire services. Save the contact information for your

country's embassy or consulate in Lisbon, should you need their assistance during your stay.

8. **Pharmacy Hours:** Many pharmacies in Lisbon close on weekends and during lunch hours. In case you need medication or medical supplies during these times, look for a "Farmácia de Serviço" (pharmacy on duty), which will be open 24/7. The location of the nearest open pharmacy will be posted on the door of any closed pharmacy.

9. **Tipping:** Tipping is appreciated but not mandatory in Lisbon. In restaurants, a tip of 10-15% is customary for good service. For taxi drivers, rounding up to the nearest euro is a polite gesture.

1.7 Practical Information

Portugal's time zone is WET (Western Europe Time) or UTC+0 (Coordinated Universal Time). During Summer, the WEST (Western Europe Summer Time) or DST (Daylight Saving Time), or UTC+1 is used.

The official hour format used in Portugal is the 24hours format. So, every hour after 12 p.m. would just go on until the 24th hour, instead of just going back to 1 p.m. This way, the official way to say the time if it is 4 p.m. would be 16h since 1 p.m. – 13h; 2 p.m. – 14h; 3 p.m. – 15h. In spite of this, in informal conversations, it is more common to use «*da manhã*» or «*da tarde/da noite*,» which translates to «**in the morning**» and «**in the afternoon,**» respectively.

Practical Information

Lisbon is a popular tourist destination that attracts visitors from all over the world. Before embarking on your journey to this historic and charming city, it's important to have a good understanding of the practical information you'll need to make your stay as comfortable and stress-free as possible.

Electricity Type

In Lisbon, the standard voltage is 230 V, and the standard frequency is 50 Hz. The plugs and sockets used are type F, which are also used in other European countries. If you're visiting from outside Europe, you'll need to bring an adapter to ensure that your electronics can be used in Lisbon.

Mobile Connectivity

Mobile connectivity in Lisbon is generally good, and most major mobile carriers have coverage throughout the city. If you're visiting from outside of Europe, be sure to check with your carrier to see if they offer international roaming, and what the associated costs are. If you don't want to incur high roaming fees, you can also purchase a local SIM card upon arrival in Lisbon.

Wifi

Wifi is widely available throughout Lisbon, and most hotels, cafes, and restaurants offer free wifi to customers. Additionally, there are many public wifi hotspots throughout the city, including in parks and other public spaces.

Lisbon Currency

Portugal's former official currency was the Escudo – PTE$. The current official currency, being part of the European Union, is the Euro – EUR€. The coins are issued in 1c, 2c, 5c, 10c, 20c, 50c, 1€ and 2€. All circulating coins have a common <u>reverse</u>, portraying a map of <u>Europe</u>, but each country in the <u>Eurozone</u> has its own design on the <u>obverse</u>, which means that each coin has a variety of different designs in circulation at once. Banknotes are issued in 5€, 10€, 20€, 50€, 100€, 200€, and 500€. Each banknote has its own color and is dedicated to an artistic period of European architecture. The front of the note features windows or gateways while the back has bridges, symbolizing links between countries and with the future.

Accommodations

Lisbon, a captivating city with a rich history and vibrant culture, offers a variety of accommodations to suit every traveler's needs and preferences. From luxury hotels with world-class amenities to charming boutique hotels reflecting the city's unique character, there's something for everyone. Here, we'll explore some recommended luxury and boutique hotels in Lisbon, including nearby attractions, websites, and approximate price ranges to help you plan your stay.

2.0 Best Areas to stay in Lisbon

Lisbon is a vibrant and diverse city that offers visitors a wide range of options when it comes to finding a place to stay. From historic neighborhoods to trendy areas filled with cafes and bars, there's something for everyone in Lisbon. In this guide, we'll take a closer look at the best areas to stay in Lisbon, based on your preferences and travel style.

Alfama

If you're looking for a quintessential Lisbon experience, Alfama is the place to be. This historic neighborhood is known for its narrow streets, charming alleyways, and stunning views of the city. It's one of the oldest neighborhoods in Lisbon, and it's full of character and charm.

Alfama is home to several famous landmarks, including the Lisbon Cathedral and São Jorge Castle. It's also a great place to experience traditional Fado music, which is a genre of music that is unique to Portugal. There are plenty of cafes and restaurants in the area, and it's a great place to stay if you want to experience the authentic side of Lisbon.

Baixa

If you're looking for a more central location, Baixa is a great option. This neighborhood is located in the heart of Lisbon, and it's home to several of the city's most famous landmarks, including Praça do Comércio and the Elevador de Santa Justa.

Baixa is a bustling and vibrant neighborhood that is full of shops, cafes, and restaurants. It's a great place to stay if you want to be close to the action and experience the city's lively atmosphere.

Chiado

Chiado is a trendy and upscale neighborhood that is known for its stylish boutiques, trendy cafes, and upscale restaurants. It's a great place to stay if you're looking for a more sophisticated and refined experience in Lisbon.

Chiado is home to several famous landmarks, including the Carmo Convent and the São Carlos Theater. It's also a great place to explore the city's vibrant arts and culture scene, with plenty of art galleries, museums, and theaters in the area.

Bairro Alto

Bairro Alto is a trendy and lively neighborhood that is known for its vibrant nightlife scene. It's a great place to stay if you want to experience Lisbon's famous bars and clubs.

During the day, Bairro Alto is a great place to explore the city's vibrant street art scene, with plenty of colorful murals and graffiti throughout the neighborhood. There are also plenty of cafes and restaurants in the area, and it's a great place to experience the city's lively and eclectic atmosphere.

Parque das Nações

If you're looking for a more modern and upscale experience in Lisbon, Parque das Nações is a great option. This neighborhood is located on the eastern side of the city, and it's home to several modern and sleek buildings, including the Lisbon Oceanarium and the Vasco da Gama Tower.

Parque das Nações is a great place to stay if you're interested in modern architecture and design, and it's a great place to explore the city's modern and innovative side.

2.1. Luxury Hotels

Four Seasons Hotel Ritz Lisbon (bit.ly/lisbonfourseasons)

Situated in the heart of Lisbon, the Four Seasons Hotel Ritz Lisbon offers elegant and spacious rooms with stunning views of the city and the Tagus River. Guests can enjoy an array of amenities, including a luxurious spa, a rooftop fitness center, and fine dining at the Varanda Restaurant. The hotel is within walking distance of the upscale Avenida da Liberdade and the historic Alfama district.

You can scan the below QR code with the camera of your mobile phone to check the prices and book the hotel:

Price range: €400-€1,200 per night, depending on the room type and season.

Pestana Palace Lisboa (bit.ly/lisbonpestanapalace)

Located in a beautifully restored 19th-century palace, the Pestana Palace Lisboa is a member of the prestigious Leading Hotels of the World group. The hotel features lush gardens, a large outdoor pool, and exquisite dining options. Nearby attractions include the Jerónimos Monastery and the Belém Tower, both UNESCO World Heritage sites.

You can scan the below QR code with the camera of your mobile phone to check the prices and book the hotel:

Price range: €250-€800 per night, depending on the room type and season.

2.2. Boutique Hotels

Santiago de Alfama (bit.ly/santiagodealfama)

Nestled in the heart of Lisbon's historic Alfama district, the Santiago de Alfama is a charming boutique hotel set in a 15th-century building. The hotel offers a blend of modern amenities and traditional Portuguese design, with each room uniquely decorated. Guests can enjoy the on-site restaurant, Café Audrey, which serves Portuguese and Mediterranean cuisine. Nearby attractions include São Jorge Castle, the Fado Museum, and the Lisbon Cathedral.

You can scan the below QR code with the camera of your mobile phone to check the prices and book the hotel:

Price range: €200-€450 per night, depending on the room type and season.

Memmo Príncipe Real (bit.ly/memmoprincipe)

Situated in the trendy Príncipe Real neighborhood, the Memmo Príncipe Real is a stylish boutique hotel offering contemporary design and stunning city views. Guests can unwind at the hotel's rooftop terrace and bar or dine at the on-site restaurant, which serves a fusion of Portuguese and international cuisine. The hotel is a short walk from the vibrant Bairro

Alto and Chiado districts, where visitors can explore a variety of shops, restaurants, and cultural attractions.

You can scan the below QR code with the camera of your mobile phone to check the prices and book the hotel:

Price range: €180-€400 per night, depending on the room type and season.

2.3. Mid-Range Hotels

Lisbon offers an array of mid-range hotels that provide comfortable accommodations, excellent service, and convenient locations without breaking the bank. Here are two recommended mid-range hotels in Lisbon, complete with nearby attractions, websites, and approximate price ranges to help you plan your stay.

Hotel Avenida Palace (bit.ly/avenidapalace)

Located in the heart of Lisbon, Hotel Avenida Palace is a historic 5-star hotel that offers a more affordable mid-range option. Set in a beautiful 19th-century building, the hotel features elegant rooms, a fitness center, and a library lounge. The hotel is steps away from the Rossio Train Station and within walking distance of the bustling Chiado district, where you'll find a variety of shops, restaurants, and cultural attractions.

You can scan the below QR code with the camera of your mobile phone to check the prices and book the hotel:

Price range: €130-€300 per night, depending on the room type and season.

TURIM Marques Hotel (bit.ly/turimmarques)

The TURIM Marques Hotel is a modern, 4-star hotel located in the Marquês de Pombal area, close to the Avenida da Liberdade. The hotel offers stylish and comfortable rooms, a 24-hour fitness center, and an on-site restaurant serving a variety of Portuguese and international dishes. Nearby attractions include the picturesque Eduardo VII Park, the Amoreiras Shopping Center, and the lively Bairro Alto district.

You can scan the below QR code with the camera of your mobile phone to check the prices and book the hotel:

Price range: €80-€200 per night, depending on the room type and season.

2.4. Budget Hotels and Hostels

Our recommended hostel to stay in Lisbon is: "Origami Lisbon Hostel."
(https://bit.ly/lisbonorigami)

Its address is Rua Álvaro Coutinho, 6, Arroios, 1150-025 Lisbon, Portugal.
Tel.: (00351) 21 824 1055

To Read Reviews of the Hotel on Booking and Book it online, go to
https://bit.ly/lisbonorigami. It has a great rating of 9.5 out of 10 in
Booking.com, and as we have used it many times, we can highly
recommend it.

You can expect to pay a price per night of 25-35€ for a double room. It is
modern, comfortable with clean and cozy rooms and it is located in
Lisbon's city center, ideal to visit various touristic attractions, as well as if
you would like to use public transportation (subway is nearby).

Another great budget option might be this hostel - Home Lisbon Hostel
(https://bit.ly/Lisbonhomehostel)

It has very positive reviews from clients worldwide and has won awards
for their quality, comfort, and sympathy.

Address: Rua São Nicolau 13, 1100-547 Lisboa | Tel: (00351) 21 888 5312 |
Price: Starting at 24€

2.5. Vacation Rentals and Apartments

Vacation rentals and apartments offer a home-away-from-home experience, providing travelers with more space, privacy, and flexibility during their stay in Lisbon. These accommodations are ideal for families, groups, or those planning an extended visit. Here are two popular platforms to find vacation rentals and apartments in Lisbon:

1. Airbnb (https://www.airbnb.com/) Airbnb offers a wide variety of unique accommodations, ranging from cozy studio apartments to spacious, fully-equipped homes. With options in every neighborhood, you can find the perfect place to suit your preferences and budget.

Price range: €40-€300 per night, depending on the property type, location, and season.

2. Vrbo (https://www.vrbo.com/) Vrbo, short for Vacation Rentals by Owner, is another popular platform for finding vacation rentals in Lisbon. The site features a selection of apartments, houses, and even unique properties like houseboats and historic buildings.

Price range: €50-€350 per night, depending on the property type, location, and season.

2.6. Unique Accommodations

or travelers seeking an unconventional lodging experience in Lisbon, the city offers a variety of unique accommodations that cater to a range of interests and tastes. Here are two noteworthy options:

The Lumiares Hotel & Spa (https://bit.ly/lisbonlumiares)

Housed in a beautifully restored 18th-century palace, The Lumiares Hotel & Spa features spacious, individually-designed apartments, blending modern amenities with the building's historic charm. Guests can enjoy a rooftop bar with panoramic city views, an on-site spa, and a restaurant specializing in Portuguese cuisine. The hotel is located in the vibrant Bairro Alto district, known for its lively nightlife, art galleries, and boutique shops.

Price range: €180-€400 per night, depending on the room type and season. Book it at https://bit.ly/lisbonlumiares

LX Factory (https://bit.ly/lisbonlxfactory)

A former industrial complex turned creative hub, LX Factory offers a unique and immersive experience for visitors looking to explore Lisbon's contemporary art and culture scene. Located in the Alcântara neighborhood, the complex features a variety of accommodations, from stylish lofts to quirky guesthouses. In addition to lodging, LX Factory is home to a range of art studios, fashion boutiques, restaurants, bars, and event spaces.

Price range: €100-€250 per night, depending on the property type and season. Book it at https://bit.ly/lisbonlxfactory

Transportation

Lisbon, a bustling city with diverse neighborhoods and historic sites, offers a variety of transportation options to help you navigate and explore its charm. From efficient public transport to taxis, ridesharing, and eco-friendly alternatives like biking and scooters, there's a mode of transportation to suit every visitor's needs. In this section, we'll provide an overview of the various ways to get around Lisbon, including websites, ticket prices, and useful tips to make your journey smooth and enjoyable.

3.1. Getting Around Lisbon

3.1.1. Public Transport

Lisbon boasts an extensive public transport system, comprising metro, buses, trams, and commuter trains. The following resources can help you plan your journey and purchase tickets:

1. **Lisbon Metro** (https://www.metrolisboa.pt/en/)

The metro is a fast and efficient way to travel within the city. There are four lines (Blue, Yellow, Green, and Red) serving the main tourist areas and connecting to major train stations. A single fare costs €1.50, while a 24-hour pass for all public transport is €6.40. You can purchase tickets at metro stations using the Viva Viagem card, a rechargeable smart card.

2. **Carris Buses and Trams** (https://www.carris.pt/en/home/)

Carris operates Lisbon's buses and the iconic yellow trams, including the famous Tram 28. Bus and tram tickets can also be loaded onto the Viva Viagem card. A single fare costs €1.50 for buses and €3.00 for trams when purchased on board or €1.34 for buses and €2.00 for trams when using the Viva Viagem card.

3. **Fertagus Trains** (https://www.fertagus.pt/en)

Fertagus operates commuter trains between Lisbon and nearby cities like Setúbal and Palmela. The fare depends on the distance traveled, with prices ranging from €1.60 to €4.55 for a single journey.

3.1.2. Taxis and Ridesharing

Taxis and ridesharing services offer a convenient way to get around Lisbon, especially for those with limited time or mobility concerns. Licensed taxis can be hailed on the street or found at designated taxi stands. Ridesharing services like Uber, Bolt, and Kapten are also popular options. Fares vary depending on distance and time of day, but a typical ride within the city center should cost around €5-€10.

3.1.3. Biking and Scooters

Lisbon's growing network of bike lanes and pedestrian-friendly streets make cycling and scooters an attractive and eco-friendly option for getting around. Several companies offer bike and e-scooter rentals, with rates starting at around €1 to unlock and €0.15-€0.20 per minute thereafter. Some popular providers include:

1. **GIRA** (https://www.gira-bicicletasdelisboa.pt/en/)

GIRA is Lisbon's public bike-sharing system, offering both regular and electric bikes. You can register online or via the app, with a 24-hour pass costing €2.

2. **Lime** (https://www.li.me/)

Lime provides electric scooters throughout Lisbon. To rent a scooter, download the app, locate a scooter nearby, and unlock it using the app.

Keep in mind that Lisbon's hilly terrain can make biking and scootering more challenging in certain areas. Always follow local traffic rules and wear a helmet for safety.

3.1.4. Car Rentals

Renting a car in Lisbon can provide you with the freedom and flexibility to explore the city and its surrounding areas at your own pace. Several international and local car rental companies operate in Lisbon, with offices at the airport, city center, and train stations. Some reputable car rental providers include:

1. Europcar (https://www.europcar.com/)

2. Avis (https://www.avis.com/)

3. Sixt (https://www.sixt.com/)

4. Hertz (https://www.hertz.com/)

Prices for car rentals vary depending on the vehicle type, rental duration, and additional services such as insurance or GPS. Expect to pay around €25-€60 per day for a compact car.

Keep in mind that driving in Lisbon can be challenging due to narrow streets, steep hills, and limited parking. Additionally, many attractions are easily accessible by public transport or on foot. Consider renting a car if you plan to explore beyond the city limits or for day trips to nearby towns and beaches.

3.1.5. Walking

Lisbon is a highly walkable city, and exploring on foot allows you to fully appreciate its charming architecture, historic neighborhoods, and vibrant street life. Many attractions are within walking distance of each other, particularly in areas like Alfama, Baixa, and Chiado.

3.2. Day Trips and Excursions

Lisbon's strategic location and excellent transportation connections make it an ideal base for exploring the surrounding regions. From UNESCO

World Heritage sites to stunning coastlines, there is a wealth of day trips and excursions to choose from, offering a diverse range of experiences to suit every traveler's interests.

3.2.1. Sintra

Sintra, a picturesque town nestled in the lush hills of the Serra de Sintra, is a must-visit destination for anyone traveling to Lisbon. With its fairy-tale palaces, historic castles, and beautiful gardens, Sintra offers a glimpse into Portugal's rich history and culture.

How to get there:

The most convenient way to reach Sintra is by train from Lisbon's Rossio Station or Oriente Station. The journey takes approximately 40 minutes, with trains running every 15-30 minutes throughout the day. A round-trip ticket costs around €4.50. You can also drive to Sintra, but be aware that parking can be challenging, especially during peak tourist season.

What to see:

1. **Pena Palace:** A colorful, romantic palace perched atop a hill, the Pena Palace is an iconic symbol of Sintra and a must-see attraction. The palace features a mix of architectural styles, including Moorish, Gothic, and Manueline influences.

2. **Moorish Castle:** The Castle of the Moors, a 9th-century fortress with stunning panoramic views, offers a glimpse into the region's rich history.

3. **Quinta da Regaleira:** This mysterious estate features a gothic palace, enchanting gardens, and the famous Initiation Well, a subterranean tower with a spiral staircase.

4. **Sintra National Palace:** Located in the heart of Sintra's historic center, this palace is known for its distinctive twin chimneys and beautifully preserved tilework.

Suggested daily itinerary:

1. Arrive in Sintra by train and start your day with a visit to the Sintra National Palace, located a short walk from the train station.

2. Take a bus or walk up the hill to the Moorish Castle, where you can explore the ruins and admire the breathtaking views of the surrounding area.

3. Continue uphill to the Pena Palace, immersing yourself in the vibrant colors and whimsical architecture of this fairy-tale castle.

4. Return to the town center and enjoy a leisurely lunch at a local restaurant.

5. After lunch, visit the enchanting Quinta da Regaleira, taking time to explore its gardens, grottoes, and the iconic Initiation Well.

6. Stroll through the charming streets of Sintra, visiting any shops or cafes that catch your eye before catching a train back to Lisbon.

This suggested itinerary offers a glimpse into the magic of Sintra, providing a memorable day trip from Lisbon. By combining historic sites, stunning architecture, and lush landscapes, Sintra showcases the beauty and diversity of Portugal's cultural heritage.

3.2.2. Cascais and Estoril

Cascais and Estoril, two charming coastal towns located along the Lisbon Riviera, offer a delightful combination of golden beaches, historic sites, and vibrant streets. With their picturesque marinas, bustling town centers, and stunning ocean views, Cascais and Estoril provide the perfect setting for a relaxing and scenic day trip from Lisbon.

How to get there:

The most convenient way to reach Cascais and Estoril is by train from Lisbon's Cais do Sodré station. The journey takes approximately 30-40 minutes, with trains running every 20 minutes throughout the day. A round-trip ticket costs around €4.50. Driving is also an option, but keep in mind that parking can be challenging during peak tourist season.

What to see:

1. **Cascais Marina:** Stroll along the marina and admire the yachts, or enjoy a drink at one of the many waterfront cafes and restaurants.

2. **Estoril Casino:** Try your luck at the largest casino in Europe, which also boasts a range of entertainment options, including concerts, shows, and art exhibitions.

3. **Boca do Inferno:** This dramatic cliff formation, known as the "Hell's Mouth," offers stunning views of the churning Atlantic Ocean.

4. **Praia do Tamariz:** Relax on this popular beach, located near the Estoril train station, and enjoy the sun, sand, and clear blue waters.

5. **Cascais Old Town:** Wander through the charming streets of Cascais's historic center, stopping at local shops, galleries, and cafes along the way.

Suggested daily itinerary:

1. Arrive in Estoril by train and start your day with a visit to the Estoril Casino, taking in the grandeur and excitement of the gaming floor.

2. Walk to Praia do Tamariz, where you can relax on the beach, swim in the ocean, or stroll along the promenade.

3. Continue along the coastal promenade to the picturesque Boca do Inferno, admiring the dramatic cliffs and stunning views of the Atlantic.

4. Head to Cascais Marina, where you can enjoy a leisurely lunch at a waterfront restaurant, taking in the views of the boats and the ocean.

5. After lunch, explore the charming streets of Cascais Old Town, visiting any shops, galleries, or cafes that catch your eye.

6. Catch a train back to Lisbon, reflecting on the beauty and charm of the Lisbon Riviera.

This suggested itinerary highlights the best of Cascais and Estoril, offering a relaxing and scenic day trip from Lisbon. With beautiful beaches, historic sites, and picturesque streets, these coastal towns showcase the allure of Portugal's stunning coastline and rich cultural heritage.

3.2.3. Óbidos

Óbidos, a picturesque medieval town located just over an hour's drive north of Lisbon, offers a delightful step back in time. With its well-preserved castle, cobblestone streets, and charming whitewashed houses adorned with colorful flowers, Óbidos provides the perfect setting for a captivating and historic day trip from Lisbon.

How to get there:

The easiest way to reach Óbidos is by car, as it offers the most flexibility in terms of timing and stops. The journey takes approximately 1-1.5 hours from Lisbon. Alternatively, you can take a bus from Lisbon's Sete Rios or Campo Grande bus stations. The journey takes around 1 hour and 40 minutes, with tickets costing around €8 each way. Another option is to join an organized tour, which often includes other nearby attractions, such as Alcobaça or Batalha.

What to see:

1. Óbidos Castle: This impressive 12th-century castle, perched on a hill overlooking the town, is a must-see attraction in Óbidos. You can explore the castle grounds and even stay overnight at the castle's hotel, Pousada Castelo de Óbidos.

2. The town walls: Walk along the well-preserved medieval walls surrounding the town, enjoying panoramic views of the surrounding countryside.

3. Rua Direita: Stroll down the town's main street, lined with charming shops, cafes, and galleries, and sample the local cherry liqueur, Ginjinha, served in chocolate cups.

4. Igreja de Santa Maria: Visit this beautiful church, which features a stunning Baroque altar and an impressive collection of 17th-century azulejo tiles.

5. Porta da Vila: Enter the town through this striking double gate, adorned with traditional blue and white azulejo tiles.

Suggested daily itinerary:

1. Arrive in Óbidos by car or bus and start your day with a visit to the impressive Óbidos Castle. Take time to explore the castle grounds and enjoy the stunning views of the town and countryside.

2. Walk along the medieval town walls, taking in the panoramic views and appreciating the town's well-preserved historic charm.

3. Descend into the town and explore Rua Direita, stopping at local shops and galleries, and sampling the famous Ginjinha liqueur in a chocolate cup.

4. Enjoy a leisurely lunch at a traditional Portuguese restaurant, savoring the local cuisine and atmosphere.

5. After lunch, visit the Igreja de Santa Maria and admire its beautiful Baroque altar and azulejo tiles.

6. Before leaving Óbidos, pass through the striking Porta da Vila and take a moment to appreciate the town's captivating beauty.

7. Return to Lisbon, reflecting on the history and charm of this enchanting medieval town.

This suggested itinerary showcases the best of Óbidos, offering a captivating and historic day trip from Lisbon. With its well-preserved castle, charming streets, and rich cultural heritage, Óbidos provides an unforgettable glimpse into Portugal's medieval past.

3.2.4. Evora

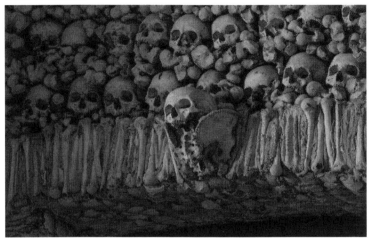

Évora, a UNESCO World Heritage-listed city located in the heart of Portugal's Alentejo region, is an enchanting destination with a rich history spanning over 2,000 years. Known for its well-preserved Roman, Moorish, and medieval architecture, as well as its vibrant cultural scene, Évora offers a fascinating and diverse day trip from Lisbon.

How to get there:

The most convenient way to reach Évora is by train from Lisbon's Oriente or Entrecampos stations. The journey takes approximately 1.5 hours, with tickets costing around €12.50 each way. Alternatively, you can drive to Évora, which takes about 1.5 hours, but parking can be limited within the city center. Organized tours are also available, which often include visits to other nearby attractions, such as Monsaraz or the Almendres Cromlech.

What to see:

1. Roman Temple of Évora: Also known as the Temple of Diana, this well-preserved Roman temple dates back to the 1st century AD and is an iconic symbol of the city.

2. Sé Cathedral of Évora: This impressive Gothic cathedral, built between the 12th and 13th centuries, features stunning views from its rooftop terrace and a beautiful collection of religious art.

3. Chapel of Bones: Located within the Church of St. Francis, this eerie chapel is lined with the bones and skulls of over 5,000 monks, serving as a reminder of the transience of life.

4. Praça do Giraldo: This bustling central square is surrounded by picturesque arcades, shops, and cafes, making it the perfect spot to relax and soak up the atmosphere.

5. University of Évora: Established in 1559, this historic university features a beautiful 18th-century main building and an impressive collection of azulejo tiles.

Suggested daily itinerary:

1. Arrive in Évora by train or car and begin your day with a visit to the Roman Temple of Évora, admiring its well-preserved columns and the surrounding views.

2. Continue to the nearby Sé Cathedral of Évora, where you can explore the impressive interior, visit the museum, and climb to the rooftop terrace for panoramic views of the city.

3. Take a short walk to the Chapel of Bones, marveling at the macabre display of human remains and reflecting on the chapel's poignant message.

4. Stroll to Praça do Giraldo and enjoy a leisurely lunch at one of the many cafes and restaurants surrounding the square.

5. After lunch, visit the University of Évora, exploring the historic main building and admiring the beautiful azulejo tiles.

6. Spend the rest of the afternoon wandering the charming streets of Évora, discovering any hidden gems, shops, or galleries that catch your eye.

7. Return to Lisbon, reflecting on the rich history and diverse architecture of this captivating city.

This suggested itinerary highlights the best of Évora, offering a fascinating and diverse day trip from Lisbon. With its impressive array of Roman, Moorish, and medieval architecture, as well as its vibrant cultural scene, Évora provides an unforgettable glimpse into the rich history and traditions of Portugal's Alentejo region.

3.2.5. The Azores and Madeira

The Azores and Madeira, two stunning archipelagos located in the Atlantic Ocean, offer a unique and unforgettable travel experience for those seeking natural beauty, adventure, and relaxation. While they are not day trip destinations from Lisbon due to their distance, they are well worth considering for an extended excursion. Each archipelago boasts its own distinct charm, landscapes, and attractions, making them ideal for exploring over a few days or even a week.

How to get there:

To reach the Azores, you can fly from Lisbon to Ponta Delgada, the main city on São Miguel Island, with a flight time of approximately 2.5 hours. The main airlines serving this route are Azores Airlines and TAP Air Portugal, with ticket prices varying depending on the season and availability.

Madeira is accessible via a 1.5-hour flight from Lisbon to Funchal, the island's capital. TAP Air Portugal and easyJet are the main airlines serving this route, with ticket prices varying according to the season and availability.

What to see in the Azores:

1. Sete Cidades: Visit the stunning twin lakes in the volcanic crater of Sete Cidades on São Miguel Island, offering breathtaking views and numerous hiking trails.

2. Furnas: Explore the geothermal wonders of Furnas, including hot springs, bubbling mud pools, and fumaroles.

3. Whale watching: Embark on a whale-watching tour to spot various species of whales and dolphins that inhabit the Azorean waters.

4. Pico Island: Climb Mount Pico, the highest peak in Portugal, for incredible views of the surrounding islands.

What to see in Madeira:

1. Funchal: Stroll through the charming streets of Funchal, visiting the bustling Mercado dos Lavradores, historic cathedrals, and lush gardens.

2. Levada walks: Explore the island's unique network of irrigation channels, known as levadas, offering scenic walking and hiking routes through Madeira's lush landscapes.

3. Cabo Girão: Stand atop one of Europe's highest sea cliffs, offering stunning views of the Atlantic Ocean and the surrounding coastline.

4. Pico do Arieiro: Hike or drive to Madeira's third-highest peak, Pico do Arieiro, for breathtaking panoramic views of the island.

Suggested multi-day itinerary:

To explore the Azores and Madeira, consider setting aside at least three to five days for each destination. This will allow you to fully experience the natural beauty, culture, and adventure these archipelagos have to offer. You can divide your time between the main islands and explore the smaller, more remote islands if time permits.

3.2.6 More Ideas

If you have an extra day or are planning on coming back, here are some suggestions you can follow, and should try to visit next time you adventure in Lisbon:

Quinta da Regaleira

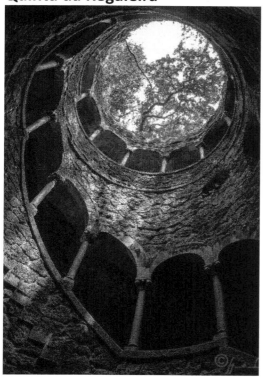

Quinta da Regaleira (http://www.serradesintra.net/quintas-de-sintra/quinta-da-regaleira) is a stunning estate located in the town of Sintra, just a short distance from Lisbon. Built in the early 20th century by a wealthy businessman and art collector, the estate is now a UNESCO World Heritage Site, drawing visitors from all over the world.

One of the most unique features of Quinta da Regaleira is its enchanting gardens, which are filled with hidden tunnels, grottos, and secret passages. Visitors can wander through the gardens and discover hidden caves, ponds, and even a small chapel. The estate's iconic Initiation Well is also a must-see attraction. This mysterious structure is a deep well with a spiral staircase that leads down to an underground chamber, creating a sense of intrigue and wonder.

In addition to the gardens, Quinta da Regaleira features a beautiful palace with ornate architecture and stunning interiors. Visitors can explore the various rooms, including the chapel, which is decorated with exquisite frescoes and stained glass windows.

Quinta da Regaleira is an ideal day trip from Lisbon, with plenty to see and do for visitors of all ages. Whether you're interested in history, architecture, or simply love exploring beautiful gardens, this estate is a must-visit destination. With its enchanting atmosphere and captivating beauty, Quinta da Regaleira is sure to leave a lasting impression on anyone who visits.

Address: Rua Barbosa do Bocage 5, 2710-567 Sintra

Opening Hours: 1st April until 30th September - 09:30am to 7pm| 1st October until a 31th March - 09:30am to 5pm

Tickets Price: Child (up to 5 years old) – Free| Young (6 - 17 years old) - 4 €| Adult (18 - 64 years old) - 6 €| Senior (65 - 79 years old) - 4 €| Senior + (from age 80) – Free|

Ericeira

Ericeira (\underline{\text{https://pt.wikipedia.org/wiki/Ericeira}}) is a charming fishing village located on the western coast of Portugal, just a short drive from Lisbon. Known for its picturesque streets, breathtaking beaches, and world-class surf, Ericeira is a popular destination for tourists and locals alike.

The village is a great place to explore on foot, with its narrow cobblestone streets and whitewashed houses adorned with colorful flowers. Visitors can stroll through the historic center and visit the town's main square, Largo dos Navegantes, which features a stunning tile mural depicting the town's maritime history.

Ericeira is also home to some of Portugal's best beaches, including Praia do Norte and Praia dos Coxos. These beaches are famous among surfers, offering some of the best waves in the country. For those who prefer a more relaxing day at the beach, Praia da Ribeira d'Ilhas is a must-visit destination. This picturesque beach is surrounded by cliffs and offers a serene and tranquil atmosphere.

In addition to its natural beauty, Ericeira is also known for its delicious seafood. The village's restaurants serve up fresh fish and seafood caught daily by local fishermen. Visitors can sample dishes like grilled sardines, octopus salad, and seafood rice, paired with a glass of local wine.

Whether you're a surfer, a foodie, or simply looking for a beautiful place to relax, Ericeira is a destination not to be missed. With its stunning beaches, charming streets, and delicious cuisine, this fishing village is sure to leave a lasting impression on anyone who visits.

Parque Natural de Monsanto

Parque Natural de Monsanto is a vast natural park that offers visitors a stunning panoramic viewpoint and terrace, among other spots that provide breathtaking views of Lisbon and its sunrise or sunset. The park is home to some of the most impressive vistas in the city, and visitors can enjoy the stunning scenery from various locations throughout the park.

Recently renovated, the park's main building is open to visitors every day, and access is free. Whether you're a nature lover, a photography enthusiast, or simply looking for a beautiful place to relax and take in the views, Parque Natural de Monsanto is a must-visit destination in Lisbon. With its impressive landscapes and stunning panoramas, this park is sure to leave a lasting impression on anyone who visits.

Adventure into the Zoo.

The Zoo of Portugal, (https://www.zoo.pt) also known as the Lisbon Zoo, is a popular attraction located in the heart of Lisbon. With over 2,000 animals from more than 300 species, this zoo offers visitors the opportunity to see a wide variety of animals up close, from elephants and giraffes to tigers and gorillas.

One of the highlights of the zoo is its impressive collection of birds, with over 200 species on display. Visitors can also see a variety of reptiles, amphibians, and insects, as well as rare and endangered animals like the Iberian lynx and the giant otter.

In addition to the animal exhibits, the zoo offers a range of activities and experiences for visitors of all ages. The zoo's dolphin show is a must-see attraction, and visitors can also take part in animal encounters and feeding sessions.

The zoo is dedicated to animal welfare and conservation, and works closely with conservation organizations and breeding programs to protect endangered species and promote biodiversity. Visitors can learn about the zoo's conservation efforts and how they can contribute to the preservation of the world's wildlife.

Overall, the Zoo of Portugal is a fun and educational destination for families, animal lovers, and anyone interested in learning more about the world's incredible diversity of wildlife. With its impressive collection of animals, engaging exhibits, and commitment to conservation, this zoo is a must-visit destination in Lisbon.

Address: Praça Marechal Humberto Delgado, 1549-004 Lisboa
Opening Hours: 21 March to 20 September - 10am to 8pm.| Last admission at 6:45pm.| 21 September to 20 March – 10am to 6pm.| Last admission at 4:45pm.

Tickets Price: Child (under 3 years) – Free| Child (3-12 years) (a) - 14,50 €| Adult (13-64 years) - 21,50 €| Senior (65 years or more) - 16 €| Group - 18 €

All the attractions and presentations are included in the entry ticket, except for the Zoo´s train. The ticket for this attraction is available only at the Train.

Galerias Romanas da Rua da Prata

These are very old and special roman caves, that are open only open three days of the year, usually around September. It is important to remember to sign up early to get a spot on the tour. Since it is open only three days a year, the tickets get sold out almost instantly once the dates are announced.

Opening Hours: Only three days a year, usually in September. (it changes every year) - 9am to 18:45pm| Tickets Price: 2€

Or if you want a little bit more fun, with some mystery and thrilling notes, try and visit these attractions:

Labririnto de Lisboa

Labirinto Lisboa (http://labirintolisboa.com/) is a unique and thrilling haunted attraction, the first of its kind in Portugal. It offers an immersive entertainment experience that combines live scare actors with special effects, across different environments, creating a winding labyrinth of dark passageways and surprising chambers. Visitors can expect a spine-tingling adventure that will leave them on the edge of their seat.

The show at Labirinto Lisboa is continuous, with no breaks or interruptions, ensuring a thrilling experience from start to finish. There is no need to book in advance, visitors can simply arrive at the attraction and purchase their tickets on the day.

Located at Rua Do Instituto Industrial 6, 1200-225 Lisboa, Labirinto Lisboa is easily accessible for visitors to the city. The attraction is open on Wednesdays, Thursdays, and Sundays from 5pm to 10pm, and on Fridays and Saturdays from 5pm to 12am. It is closed on Mondays and Tuesdays.

Ticket prices for Labirinto Lisboa vary depending on the type of ticket chosen. A normal ticket costs 15€, while the Grand Master and Fast Pass tickets are priced at 25€. For groups, a 10% discount is available on tickets, bringing the price down to 13,50€ per person.

Lisbon Escape Game

The Lisbon Escape Game(http://www.lisbonescapegame.com/) is an exciting and challenging real-life game that will put your problem-solving skills to the test. The goal is to escape from a room within a set time limit of one hour by finding and using real objects, solving puzzles, decoding messages, and combining a series of clues to unlock the way out. This game is designed for teams of 2 to 6 people, and if you have more than 6 players, two games can be played simultaneously for up to 12 players.

To participate in the Lisbon Escape Game, visitors must first book an available time slot through the online booking system on their website. Once a booking has been made, an email will be sent with instructions on how to pay and how to prepare for the game.

Located at Rua da Padaria 25, 1100-016 Lisboa, the Lisbon Escape Game is easily accessible for visitors to the city. It is open every day from 12pm to 11pm, allowing visitors to choose a time that works best for them.

Ticket prices for the Lisbon Escape Game are 70€ per group, making it an affordable and fun activity for friends, family, or coworkers. Overall, the Lisbon Escape Game is a must-try experience for those looking for a unique and challenging adventure in Lisbon.

Food and Dining

4.1. Portuguese Cuisine

4.1.1. Must-Try Dishes

In Portugal, codfish is used in innumerous dishes, and it is seen as the country's food symbol. However, Portuguese gastronomy is much more than just the "Bacalhau." Portugal's cuisine is very rich and diverse, and there are many typical and incomparable meals you most definitely have to try while you are here.

Below, there will be a few examples of local dishes that you should taste to enhance your culinary experience, while you are in Lisbon. Some of them are typical from many different parts of Portugal, and not particularly Lisbon. Nevertheless, you will find suggestions of some of the places you could visit to eat these specialties as if you were in the city they originated from. Enjoy!

1. **Pastel De Nata [Portuguese]: Custard Pie**

The Pastel de Belém was elected, in 2011, as one of the 7 Wonders of Gastronomy (https://pt.wikipedia.org/wiki/Sete_maravilhas_da_gastronomia) of Portugal. As mentioned above, the original recipe is still a secret very well kept by the first pastry shop that sold these. Situated in Belém, Pastéis de Belém (http://pasteisdebelem.pt/)offers the most original and traditional pastel de nata there is. They are served hot out of the baking oven, with cinnamon and powdered sugar on top. Only the ones that come from this shop may be called Pastéis de Belém. All the others are merely pastéis de nata. In spite of this, currently, there is an increasing number of pastry shops recreating this unique delicacy, and successfully. Now, you can find it in any coffee shop throughout Portugal, and even abroad. Some of them even compete with the original for the tastiest pastel de nata there is.

Best places to savor them:
Pastéis de Belém (http://pasteisdebelem.pt/)
Address: Rua de Belém 84-92, 1300-085 Lisboa | Opening Hours: 8am to 11pm – Open everyday

Pastelaria Alcôa (http://www.pastelaria-alcoa.com/)
Address: Rua Garrett 37, 1200-309 Lisboa | Opening Hours: 9am to 10pm – Open everyday

Manteigaria - Fábrica de Pastéis de Nata (https://www.zomato.com/pt/manteigaria)
Address: Rua do Loreto 2, 1200-108 Lisboa | Opening Hours: 8am to 12am – Open everyday

2. Travesseiro de Sintra [Portuguese]: Sintra's Pillow

One of the main delicacies Sintra is known for. Every year, millions of tourists, and Portuguese, visit the famous "Piriquita" to try one of these, but there are currently shops in the Lisbon center that sell this pastry.

Casa da Piriquita, (https://piriquita.pt/) Address: Rua Padarias 1, 2710-533 Sintra

<u>Piriquita II , (https://piriquita.pt/)</u>**Address:** Rua das Padarias 18, 2710-533 Sintra| Opening Hours: Sunday to Monday – 8:30am to 8pm, Tuesday – Closed

Fábrica de Queijadas – Recordação de Sintra no Mercado da Ribeira

Address: 481, Av. 24 de Julho, Lisboa| Opening Hours: Monday, Tuesday, Wednesday, Sunday – 10am to 12am| Thursday, Friday, Saturday – 10am to 2am.

3. **Queijadas** [Portuguese]:

Queijada is another pastry famously made in Sintra. It has many variations currently, but originaly its recipe consists of cheese, eggs, milk, and sugar.

<u>Fábrica de Queijadas – Recordação de Sintra:</u>
<u>(http://queijadasintra.wixsite.com/recordacaodesintra)</u>

Address: Av. Dom Francisco de Almeida 31, 2710-431 Sintra| **Opening Hours:** <u>Monday to Saturday</u> – 8am to 4:30pm | <u>Sunday</u> – Closed

Fábrica de Queijadas – Recordação de Sintra no Mercado da Ribeira:

Address: Av. 24 de Julho, 481, Lisboa| **Opening Hours:** <u>Sunday to Wednesday</u> – 10am to 12am| <u>Thursday to Saturday</u> – 10am to 2am

4. Cozido à Portuguesa [Portuguese]: Portuguese Stew

Cozido à Portuguesa, or Portuguese Stew, is a traditional and hearty dish that showcases the rich flavors and culinary diversity of Portugal. This beloved meal is composed of a variety of meats, such as beef, pork, and chicken, alongside regional sausages like chouriço and morcela, all slow-cooked to tender perfection.

The dish also features an assortment of vegetables, including potatoes, carrots, turnips, and cabbage, which absorb the delicious flavors of the meats and sausages as they cook. Each region of Portugal adds its unique touch to the recipe, often incorporating local ingredients and cooking methods. Cozido à Portuguesa is typically enjoyed as a family meal, bringing people together to savor the warmth and comfort of this quintessential Portuguese dish.

Zé do Cozido (http://www.zedocozido.pt/) - Visit this restaurant to try their famous "cozido à portuguesa".

Address: Rua José Acúrcio das Neves 3, 1900-221 Lisboa| **Opening Hours:** Closed on Saturdays

7. Caldo Verde [Portuguese]: Green Broth

A very popular soup in Portugal with chorizo and potatoes, collard greens, olive oil and salt!

8. Arroz-doce [Portuguese]: Rice Pudding

A sweet dessert made of rice, milk, eggs and lemon zest!

9.Bacalhau à Zé do Pipo [Pt]: Cod, in Ze do Pipo Style

Bacalhau à Zé do Pipo, or Cod in Ze do Pipo Style, is a classic Portuguese dish that celebrates the country's love affair with bacalhau, or salted cod.

This flavorful recipe is named after a famous tavern owner from Porto, Zé do Pipo, who was known for his delectable cod creations. The dish features tender flakes of salted cod that are cooked and then mixed with sautéed onions and garlic. The cod mixture is then topped with a layer of smooth and creamy mashed potatoes, which are often piped into elegant patterns for an attractive presentation. The dish is finished with a garnish of black olives and a sprinkling of paprika before being baked in the oven until golden and bubbly. Bacalhau à Zé do Pipo is a rich and comforting meal that showcases the versatility and enduring popularity of salted cod in Portuguese cuisine.

10. Queijo Serra da Estrela [Pt]: Serra Da Estrela Cheese

Queijo Serra da Estrela, or Serra da Estrela Cheese, is a prized artisanal cheese originating from the Serra da Estrela region in central Portugal. This delectable cheese is made from the raw milk of Bordaleira sheep, a breed native to the area, and boasts a unique combination of flavors and textures. With a slightly crumbly yet creamy consistency, Queijo Serra da Estrela is known for its distinctive, tangy taste that comes from the use of cardoon thistle as a coagulant, rather than traditional rennet. The cheese is typically aged for a minimum of 30 days, although some variations can be aged for up to several months, resulting in a stronger flavor and firmer texture. Often enjoyed on its own or with a slice of fresh bread, Queijo Serra da Estrela is a delicious and authentic representation of Portugal's rich cheese-making tradition.

11. **Ovos Moles de Aveiro** [Pt], Soft Eggs from Aveiro [En]

These soft eggs are a local delicacy from Aveiro and are made only of egg yolks and sugar. After that, the mixture is put inside of a small rice paper casing in nautical shapes, such as shells or fish. Try them here in Lisbon:

Casa dos Ovos Moles em Lisboa
(https://www.casadosovosmolesemlisboa.pt/)

Address: Calçada da Estrela 142, 1200-666 Lisboa| **Opening Hours:** Tuesday to Sunday – 11am to 7pm, Monday - Closed

12. Peixinhos da Horta [Pt], Peixinhos da Horta (Tempura) [En]

Peixinhos da Horta, or Tempura Green Beans, is a delightful Portuguese appetizer that showcases the country's culinary ingenuity and fusion of flavors. The name "Peixinhos da Horta" translates to "little fish from the garden," a playful reference to the appearance of the green beans, which resemble small, colorful fish when coated in the crispy batter. This traditional dish is believed to have inspired the Japanese tempura technique, introduced by Portuguese missionaries and traders in the 16th century. To prepare Peixinhos da Horta, fresh green beans are dipped in a light and airy batter made from flour, water, and sometimes egg, before being deep-fried to golden perfection. The resulting dish is a delicious combination of tender, flavorful green beans encased in a crisp, delicate coating. Peixinhos da Horta is a popular appetizer or side dish in Portugal, enjoyed with a squeeze of lemon and often accompanied by a flavorful dipping sauce.

13. Caldeirada de Peixe [Pt], Portuguese Fish Stew [En]

Caldeirada de Peixe, or Portuguese Fish Stew, is a mouthwatering dish that pays homage to Portugal's abundant seafood offerings and coastal heritage. This aromatic and comforting stew features a medley of fish and shellfish, such as white fish, monkfish, shrimp, and clams, combined with a rich, flavorful broth made from tomatoes, onions, garlic, bell peppers, and white wine. Herbs like parsley, cilantro, and bay leaves are added to enhance the depth of flavors, while potatoes are included to provide heartiness and substance.

The dish is typically slow-cooked to allow the various ingredients to meld together, creating a harmonious and satisfying meal. Caldeirada de Peixe is often enjoyed with a side of crusty bread, perfect for sopping up the delicious, savory broth. This traditional Portuguese dish showcases the country's love of seafood and its ability to transform simple, fresh ingredients into a delectable and soul-warming culinary experience.

14. Tosta Mista [Portuguese]:

A tosta mista is a ham and cheese sandwich pressed together, making the cheese melt, and with a lot of salted butter on it. You can find on every coffee shop in Lisbon or Portugal.

15. Bifana [Portuguese]:

Bifana, a simple yet beloved Portuguese sandwich, is a testament to the country's ability to create culinary magic with just a few humble ingredients. This iconic street food features a tender, thinly-sliced pork cutlet marinated in a flavorful blend of garlic, white wine, paprika, and sometimes piri-piri sauce for an added kick. The marinated pork is then quickly pan-fried, allowing it to absorb the aromatic flavors while remaining juicy and succulent.

The cooked pork is nestled between two slices of crusty bread, often a soft, slightly toasted Portuguese roll known as a "papo-seco." The sandwich is sometimes garnished with mustard, mayonnaise, or a simple tomato and lettuce combo, but the star of the show is undoubtedly the savory, seasoned pork. Bifanas can be found at street food vendors, cafes, and snack bars across Portugal, providing a delicious and satisfying meal that is perfect for enjoying on-the-go or as a quick, comforting snack.

4.1.2. Traditional Pastries

Portugal's rich history of baking and pastry-making has given rise to an incredible variety of traditional pastries that are both visually appealing and delightfully delicious. Some of the most iconic Portuguese pastries include:

Pastel de Nata: Also known as Pastéis de Belém, these irresistible egg custard tarts feature a flaky, buttery crust filled with a creamy, sweet custard and are lightly dusted with cinnamon and powdered sugar.

Travesseiros de Sintra: These pillow-shaped pastries from Sintra are made with puff pastry and filled with a sweet almond and egg yolk cream, creating a delicate and flavorful treat.

Queijadas de Évora: Hailing from the town of Évora, these small, round pastries consist of a thin crust filled with a mixture of fresh cheese, sugar, eggs, and cinnamon, offering a delightful balance of sweet and savory flavors.

Ovos Moles: A specialty from Aveiro, Ovos Moles are made from a combination of egg yolks and sugar, encased in a delicate, rice paper-like wafer, often molded into various shapes, such as shells or fish.

4.1.3. Wine and Beverages

Portugal boasts a long tradition of wine-making and offers a diverse selection of high-quality wines and beverages that pair wonderfully with its rich and varied cuisine. Some notable Portuguese wines and beverages include:

Vinho Verde: Literally translated as "green wine," Vinho Verde is a young, refreshing white wine that is slightly effervescent and often characterized by its crisp, fruity, and slightly acidic profile. Our suggestion is to try the **Alvarinho Quintas Melgaço – Verde Branco**. The bottle is around 9€.

Port Wine: Originating from the Douro Valley, Port Wine is a world-renowned fortified wine that is typically sweet, rich, and high in alcohol content. It is available in various styles, including Ruby, Tawny, and Vintage Port, and is often enjoyed as a dessert wine or digestif.

Madeira Wine: Produced on the island of Madeira, this unique fortified wine is known for its complex flavors and remarkable aging potential. It is available in a range of styles, from dry to sweet, and is often used as an aperitif, dessert wine, or cooking ingredient.

Ginjinha: A popular cherry liqueur native to Portugal, Ginjinha is made from sour cherries infused with sugar, water, and alcohol, resulting in a sweet and slightly tart beverage that is often enjoyed as a digestif or festive drink.

4.2. Restaurants

Lisbon offers a diverse array of dining options, ranging from sophisticated fine dining establishments to casual restaurants and traditional tascas. The city's gastronomic scene is a reflection of Portugal's rich culinary history, showcasing the flavors, techniques, and ingredients that have shaped the nation's cuisine over the centuries. Whether you're seeking a luxurious dining experience or a laid-back, authentic meal, Lisbon has something to suit every palate and preference.

4.2.1. Fine Dining

Lisbon's fine dining scene has flourished in recent years, with numerous Michelin-starred restaurants and upscale establishments providing unforgettable culinary experiences. Some noteworthy fine dining options in Lisbon include:

Belcanto (https://www.belcanto.pt/):

Awarded two Michelin stars, Belcanto is helmed by celebrated chef José Avillez and offers contemporary interpretations of traditional Portuguese dishes using innovative techniques and premium ingredients.

Alma (https://www.almalisboa.pt/pt):

Led by renowned chef Henrique Sá Pessoa, Alma holds one Michelin star and focuses on creative, modern Portuguese cuisine, showcasing the best of the country's culinary heritage in a refined and elegant setting.

Loco (https://www.loco.pt/):

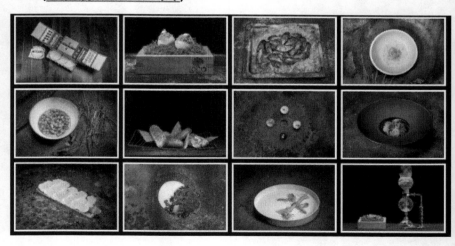

With one Michelin star, Loco is known for its avant-garde approach to Portuguese gastronomy, offering a tasting menu that pushes the boundaries of traditional flavors and techniques.

4.2.2. Casual Restaurants and Tascas

For those seeking a more relaxed and authentic dining experience, Lisbon is home to a plethora of casual restaurants and traditional tascas, where you can enjoy delicious, home-style Portuguese fare in a warm and welcoming atmosphere. Some popular options include:

Cervejaria Ramiro (https://www.cervejariaramiro.com):

A Lisbon institution, Cervejaria Ramiro is renowned for its incredible seafood, including fresh clams, crab, and the famous giant tiger prawns. This lively, bustling eatery provides a genuine taste of Portuguese seafood culture.

O Piteu da Graça (https://www.restauranteopiteu.pt/):

Located in the historic Graça neighborhood, O Piteu da Graça is a charming tasca known for its delicious traditional dishes, such as Bacalhau à Brás, Arroz de Pato, and Cozido à Portuguesa.

Taberna da Rua das Flores (https://tberna.com/) :

This cozy tavern offers a seasonal menu of Portuguese petiscos (small plates) and larger dishes, showcasing the best of regional produce and traditional flavors in a relaxed and convivial setting.

4.2.3. Seafood Restaurants

Lisbon's coastal location provides access to an abundance of fresh seafood, which is celebrated in the city's numerous seafood restaurants. Some popular seafood dining options in Lisbon include:

Cervejaria Ramiro (website: cervejariaramiro.pt, price range: $$-$$$): As mentioned earlier, this iconic Lisbon eatery is known for its extensive selection of top-quality seafood, from clams and oysters to crab and lobster.

A Cevicheria (website: acevicheria.pt, price range: $$-$$$):

Focusing on Peruvian-inspired seafood dishes, A Cevicheria offers a variety of ceviche options as well as other seafood specialties, all made with the freshest ingredients.

Marisqueira Uma (website: https://umamarisqueira.com/, price range: $$$-$$$$): This upscale seafood restaurant is renowned for its expertly prepared shellfish, including crab, shrimp, and a variety of clams, as well as other seafood dishes like grilled fish and rice dishes.

4.2.4. Vegetarian and Vegan Options

Lisbon's dining scene has embraced the growing demand for vegetarian and vegan cuisine, with several establishments dedicated to plant-based dining. Some notable vegetarian and vegan-friendly restaurants in Lisbon include:

The Food Temple (website: https://www.facebook.com/FoodTemple/ , price range: $-$$): Located in the Mouraria district, The Food Temple offers a changing menu of creative vegetarian and vegan dishes made from local, seasonal ingredients.

Terra (website: linktr.ee/terralisboa, price range: $$-$$$): This vegetarian restaurant features a delicious buffet of international and Portuguese-inspired dishes, with a focus on fresh, organic produce and a beautiful outdoor garden setting.

Jardim das Cerejas (website: facebook.com/jardimdascerejas, price range: $-$$):

Vegan restaurant in the heart of Lisbon's downtown

This popular vegan eatery in Chiado offers a daily buffet of flavorful plant-based dishes, including soups, salads, and main courses, as well as a selection of vegan desserts.

4.2.5. International Cuisine

Lisbon's cosmopolitan atmosphere and diverse population have given rise to a vibrant international dining scene. Some of the city's best international cuisine options include:

A Valenciana (website: https://www.restauranteavalenciana.pt/ , price range: $$-$$$): This popular restaurant specializes in Portuguese-style grilled chicken with piri-piri sauce, but also offers a variety of international dishes, such as Brazilian-style grilled meats and African-inspired stews.

Boa-Bao (website: https://www.boabao.pt/ , price range: $$-$$$):

Boa-Bao serves up flavorful Pan-Asian cuisine in a stylish and relaxed setting, offering dishes from Thailand, Vietnam, Malaysia, and more.

4.3. Food Markets and Street Food

Lisbon's food markets and street food vendors provide visitors with the opportunity to sample a wide variety of Portuguese flavors and dishes in a casual and lively setting. Some must-visit food markets and street food destinations in the city include:

Mercado da Ribeira (Time Out Market): This bustling food market, curated by Time Out magazine, brings together a diverse selection of

Lisbon's best restaurants, bars, and food stalls under one roof. Visitors can sample everything from traditional Portuguese dishes to international cuisine, all while enjoying a vibrant and communal atmosphere.

Feira da Ladra: Lisbon's oldest flea market, Feira da Ladra, also features a variety of street food vendors offering delicious local snacks, such as bifanas, pastéis de nata, and grilled sardines.

Mercado de Campo de Ourique: This neighborhood market in Campo de Ourique offers a mix of fresh produce, gourmet food products, and food stalls serving a variety of Portuguese and international dishes in a relaxed, family-friendly environment.

4.4. Coffee Shops and Cafés

Lisbon is known for its vibrant café culture, with numerous coffee shops and traditional pastelarias (pastry shops) offering a delightful array of pastries, sandwiches, and coffee beverages. Some must-visit coffee shops and cafés in Lisbon include:

1. **Pastéis de Belém:** As the birthplace of the famous Pastel de Nata, Pastéis de Belém is a must-visit for anyone with a sweet tooth. Enjoy the iconic egg custard tart alongside a bica (Portuguese espresso) in this historic café, which has been serving customers since 1837.

2. **Fábrica Coffee Roasters:** This specialty coffee shop sources and roasts its own beans, offering expertly brewed coffee in a modern, industrial setting. Fábrica Coffee Roasters has multiple locations throughout the city, making it easy to find a spot to enjoy a perfectly crafted espresso or cappuccino.

3. **A Brasileira:** One of Lisbon's most famous and historic cafés, A Brasileira has been a gathering place for artists, writers, and intellectuals since 1905. Enjoy a traditional Portuguese coffee or a light snack in this beautifully preserved café, which features an iconic bronze statue of the poet Fernando Pessoa.

4.5. Bars and Nightlife

Lisbon's nightlife scene is renowned for its diversity and vibrancy, with a plethora of bars, clubs, and music venues that cater to a wide range of tastes and preferences. Whether you're seeking a sophisticated cocktail lounge, a lively dance club, or a cozy neighborhood bar, Lisbon has something to offer. Here are some must-visit bars and nightlife destinations in the city:

1. **Park** (website: https://www.lisbonlux.com/lisbon-bars/park.html):

Located on the rooftop of a parking garage in Bairro Alto, Park offers stunning views of the city skyline and a relaxed, open-air atmosphere. The bar serves creative cocktails and light bites, making it a popular spot for a sunset drink or late-night gathering.

2. **Pensão Amor** (website: pensaoamor.com):

Housed in a former brothel in the trendy Cais do Sodré district, Pensão Amor is a quirky and eclectic bar that features vintage decor and a lively atmosphere. Enjoy a drink in the cozy lounge or catch a show in the intimate theater.

3. **Lux Frágil** (website: luxfragil.com): A Lisbon nightlife institution, Lux Frágil is a sprawling club that features multiple dance floors, a riverside terrace, and a diverse lineup of local and international DJs. Dress to impress and be prepared to dance the night away.

4. **Foxtrot** (website: https://www.barfoxtrot.pt/):

This speakeasy-style bar in the Chiado district is hidden behind a bookcase and offers a cozy and intimate setting for enjoying expertly crafted cocktails. The menu features classic and creative drinks made with premium spirits and fresh ingredients.

5. **Red Frog Speakeasy** (website: redfrog.pt): Another speakeasy-style bar, Red Frog is located in the historic Bairro Alto neighborhood and offers a retro-inspired setting and expertly crafted cocktails. To enter the bar, visitors must find the hidden door and speak the password to the doorman.

Events and Festivals

Lisbon is a city that loves to celebrate, with a vibrant calendar of events and festivals that take place throughout the year. From traditional cultural celebrations to music festivals, film events, and more, there's always something happening in Lisbon. Here are some of the city's most popular events and festivals:

5.1. Traditional Festivals

Lisbon has a rich cultural heritage that is celebrated through a variety of traditional festivals and events. Some of the most notable include:

1. **Festa de Santo António**: This annual festival, held in June, is a celebration of Lisbon's patron saint, Santo António. The festival features parades, street parties, and traditional foods, such as sardines and caldo verde soup.

2. **Festas de Lisboa**: A month-long series of events and activities that take place throughout the city in June, including music concerts, theater performances, and street parties.

3. **Carnaval**: Lisbon's Carnaval celebrations are known for their colorful parades and lively street parties, with events taking place throughout the city in February or March.

5.2. Music Festivals and Concerts

Lisbon is a city that loves music, with a vibrant music scene that is reflected in a number of festivals and concerts throughout the year. Some popular music events in Lisbon include:

1. **NOS Alive (https://nosalive.com/):** One of Portugal's largest music festivals, NOS Alive features a lineup of international and local artists across multiple stages, held in July at Passeio Marítimo de Algés.

2. **Super Bock Super Rock (https://superbocksuperrock.pt/):** A three-day festival held in July at Meco beach, Super Bock Super Rock features a lineup of alternative and indie rock bands from around the world.

3. **Jazz em Agosto (https://gulbenkian.pt/jazzemagosto/en/)** Held in August at the Calouste Gulbenkian Foundation, Jazz em Agosto is an annual jazz festival that features a diverse range of international jazz musicians.

5.3. Film and Theater Events

Lisbon's cultural scene also includes a variety of film and theater events, showcasing the city's creative spirit and artistic talents. Some notable events in Lisbon include:

Lisbon & Sintra Film Festival: Held annually in November, the Lisbon & Sintra Film Festival features a diverse lineup of international films and includes Q&A sessions with filmmakers and actors.

Festival de Almada: An annual theater festival held in Almada, just south of Lisbon, featuring local and international theater productions.

Teatro Nacional D. Maria II: Lisbon's National Theater offers a year-round program of performances, including plays, dance productions, and music concerts.

5.4. Sports and Competitions

Lisbon is home to a number of sports events and competitions, showcasing the city's passion for sports and athleticism. Some notable events include:

Lisbon Half Marathon (https://www.running-portugal.com/lisbon/lisbonhalf/en/home.html): Held annually in

March, the Lisbon Half Marathon attracts thousands of runners from around the world for a scenic race through the city's historic center.

Estoril Open (https://www.atptour.com/en/tournaments/estoril/7290/overview): A prestigious tennis tournament held in April or May at the Estoril Tennis Club, featuring some of the world's top players.

Lisbon International Triathlon (https://worldtriathlonlisbon.com): A popular triathlon held in May that includes a 1.5-kilometer swim, a 40-kilometer bike ride, and a 10-kilometer run through the city.

5.5. Art and Cultural Events
Lisbon is a city that celebrates art and culture, with a variety of events and festivals that showcase the city's creative spirit and heritage. Some popular art and cultural events in Lisbon include:

ARCOlisboa: An international contemporary art fair held annually in May, featuring works from leading galleries and artists from around the world.

Festival Internacional de Música de Marvão: Held in July in the historic town of Marvão, the International Music Festival features classical music concerts in stunning medieval venues.

DocLisboa (https://doclisboa.org/): A documentary film festival held annually in October that features a diverse range of international documentaries and includes Q&A sessions with filmmakers and experts.

Insider Tips and Recommendations

Lisbon is a city that is rich in history, culture, and beauty, with a vibrant community and a lively spirit. To get the most out of your visit to Lisbon, consider exploring some of the city's hidden gems and off-the-beaten-path experiences. Here are some insider tips and recommendations to help you discover the best of Lisbon:

6.1. Hidden Gems and Off-the-Beaten-Path Experiences

LX Factory:

Located in the Alcântara neighborhood, LX Factory is a vibrant hub of creative and cultural activity. This former industrial complex has been transformed into a dynamic space that features art galleries, design shops, restaurants, and bars. Visitors can explore the various buildings and discover the unique and eclectic offerings that make LX Factory a must-visit destination.

Miradouro da Senhora do Monte:

For stunning views of Lisbon's skyline and an off-the-beaten-path experience, head to Miradouro da Senhora do Monte. This hilltop lookout point offers breathtaking views of the city and is a great spot for a picnic or a romantic sunset stroll.

Casa dos Bicos:

This historic building in the Alfama neighborhood is a hidden gem that is often overlooked by tourists. Casa dos Bicos, or House of the Spikes, was built in the 16th century and features a distinctive façade of diamond-shaped stones. The building now houses the José Saramago Foundation, a cultural center that honors the life and work of the Nobel Prize-winning author.

Mercado de Campo de Ourique:

While Lisbon's Time Out Market is a popular destination for foodies, Mercado de Campo de Ourique offers a more authentic and local experience. This neighborhood market features a mix of fresh produce, gourmet food products, and food stalls serving a variety of Portuguese and international dishes in a relaxed, family-friendly environment.

São Jorge Castle:

While São Jorge Castle is a well-known attraction, visitors can avoid the crowds and get a more intimate experience by visiting early in the morning or just before closing time. This historic castle offers stunning views of the city and a glimpse into Lisbon's rich past.

6.2. Sustainable Travel and Responsible Tourism

As a responsible traveler, it's important to be aware of your impact on the environment and local communities. Fortunately, Lisbon has a number of sustainable and eco-friendly initiatives in place that make it easy to travel responsibly. Here are some tips for sustainable travel and responsible tourism in Lisbon:

1.   Use public transportation: Lisbon's public transportation system is efficient and affordable, making it a great option for getting around the city while reducing your carbon footprint.

2.   Choose eco-friendly accommodations: There are a number of hotels and accommodations in Lisbon that prioritize sustainability and eco-

friendliness, such as the Inspira Santa Marta Hotel and the Memmo Alfama Hotel.

3. Support local businesses: By supporting local restaurants, shops, and vendors, you can contribute to the local economy and reduce your impact on the environment by avoiding large chain stores and restaurants.

4. Reduce waste: Lisbon has a number of waste reduction initiatives in place, such as recycling and composting programs. Make an effort to reduce your waste while traveling by bringing a reusable water bottle, saying no to plastic straws, and properly disposing of your trash.

5. Respect local culture and traditions: As a responsible traveler, it's important to respect the local culture and traditions of the places you visit. Be mindful of dress codes, language, and customs, and avoid activities that exploit animals or harm the environment.

6.3. LGBTQ+ Friendly Travel Resources

Lisbon is a city that is known for its LGBTQ+ friendliness and acceptance, with a thriving LGBTQ+ community and a number of resources and accommodations available for LGBTQ+ travelers. Here are some tips for LGBTQ+ friendly travel in Lisbon:

Seek out LGBTQ+ friendly accommodations: There are a number of hotels and accommodations in Lisbon that are LGBTQ+ friendly, such as the Memmo Príncipe Real Hotel and the My Rainbow Rooms Gay Men's Guest House.

Visit LGBTQ+ friendly areas: Lisbon has several neighborhoods that are known for their LGBTQ+ friendliness and community, such as the Príncipe Real and Bairro Alto neighborhoods.

Attend LGBTQ+ events: Lisbon hosts a number of LGBTQ+ events throughout the year, such as the Lisbon Pride Parade and the Queer Lisboa Film Festival.

Seek out resources: There are several resources available for LGBTQ+ travelers in Lisbon, such as the Lisbon Gay Circuit website and the Lisbon Tourist Office's LGBTQ+ guide.

3-Day Itinerary: Classic Lisbon

Welcome to Lisbon, Portugal's vibrant and historic capital city! With its rich cultural heritage, stunning architecture, and delicious cuisine, Lisbon is a must-visit destination for travelers seeking an authentic European experience. In this 3-day itinerary, we'll take you on a journey through classic Lisbon, highlighting the city's most iconic landmarks and hidden gems. From the historic Alfama neighborhood to the lively Bairro Alto district, get ready to fall in love with all that Lisbon has to offer. So, grab your walking shoes and let's explore the best of classic Lisbon!

Day 1: Arrival, Top Monuments

09:45

Arrival at the Portela Airport – Lisbon International Airport (https://www.aeroportolisboa.pt/en/lis/home), which is ideally located just outside the city center.

That is the only airport in Lisbon and the biggest airport in Portugal. It has two different terminals, Terminal 1 and Terminal 2, where the second one is mostly used by low-cost airlines, such as Ryanair, easyJet or Transavia, among others.

09:55

Take the luggage and pass through passport control.

If you arrive in Terminal 1, It does not take more than 10-15 minutes to go through the baggage claim area and exit to the arrival's terminal (depending on where your plane parks), especially if you are traveling only with a hand/cabin luggage, something very common in low-cost airlines. However, if you arrive in Terminal 2, it could take between 20-25 minutes, since the bus journey to Terminal 1, where the baggage claim area is located, could take an additional 5-10 minutes.

You have several options to choose from to head into the city. You can take the metro, bus, shuttle, uber/taxi, rent a car or a motorcycle from the airport to the city center, to go to the hotel. The Hotel for this itinerary is "Origami Lisbon Hostel", but you can adapt for any hotel you choose to stay.

View *ZoomTip 1.1*

Prices:

- **Metro:** 1,40€ + 0,50€ for Viva Viagem Electronic Card (rechargeable) (21 minutes)
- **Bus:** 1,80€ + 0,50€ for Viva Viagem Electronic Card (rechargeable) (40 minutes)
- **Shuttle:** 3,50€ (25-30 minutes)
- **Uber/Taxi:** Varying fare
- **Emov:** 0,18€/min
- **eCooltra**: 0,24€/min

10:40

Accommodate in the hotel and then visit the top monuments on foot

Help yourself in the hotel and then start your day visiting some of the top Lisbon monuments. We highly recommend you begin your journey at the beginning of Liberty Avenue (*Avenida da Liberdade*), near *Marquês de Pombal* statue, making your way to the city center (Rossio Square and Commerce Square areas) where you will pass by the stunning Santa Justa Lift. It is the best way to get to know the city on your first day.

View *ZoomTip 1.2*

12:45

Take a first look at Lisbon's skyline and historic buildings from the remarkable Santa Justa Lift, in the middle of Lisbon's city center.

View *ZoomTip 1.2* | **Ticket Price:** 1,5€

14:00

Lunch at Restaurant Bonjardim

Adress: Tv. De Santo Antão, 11, 1150-312 Lisboa | **Tel:** (00351) 21 342 4389

Don't lose the opportunity to eat one of the best chicken dishes of your life! The Portuguese way to cook chicken is called *Frango de Churrasco* and this is the place of election to do so since it is around for decades!

Price: 8€ - 12€ per person

16:00

Visit the St. George's Castle *(Castelo de São Jorge)*, one of the most iconic places in Portugal's capital city.

View *ZoomTip 1.2* | **Ticket Price:** 8,5€ (Students < 25 years old: 5€)

18:00

Visit the Cathedral of Lisbon *(Sé de Lisboa)*.

View *ZoomTip 1.2* | **Ticket Price:** Free

20:00

Dinner at Time Out Mercado da Ribeira, an outstanding place in an entirely different environment!

View *ZoomTip 1.3* | **Price:** 10€ - 20€ per person.

22:00

Grab a metro back to your hotel and rest.

1st Day in Lisbon – Map

You can get the google maps with all the suggested places for the first day of your itinerary, at https://bit.ly/lisbondayone

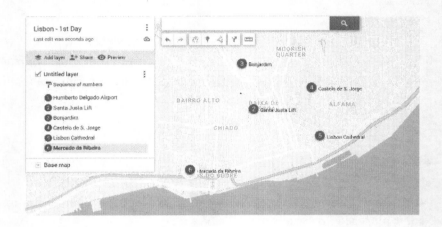

ZoomTip 1.1 Transportation

When it comes to reaching the city center, Lisbon offers several transportation options, and luckily, the airport is relatively close compared to other European cities. The choice of how to get there depends on your budget and the time you have available for your journey. However, without a doubt, the Metro stands out as the most convenient and efficient mode of transport to reach almost any destination in Lisbon. Let's explore the details of each available option:

From Portela Airport – Lisbon International Airport to city center

METRO:

- Working Hours: 6:30 am – 1:00 am
- Price: 1,40€ + 0,50€ for Viva Viagem Electronic Card (rechargeable)
- Average Journey Time: 21 minutes
- Hotel Nearest Stop: Anjos (200 m) or Intendente (350 m)

BUS:

Working Hours:

- **Nº 208:** Cais Sodré – Airport – Oriente Station (daily - operates between 12:30 am and 5:35 am)
- **Nº 705:** Oriente Station – Airport – Roma Station / Areeiro (work days only)
- **Nº 722:** Praça Londres – Airport – Portela (every day)
- **Nº 744:** Marquês Pombal – Airport – Moscavide (every day)
- **Nº 783:** Amoreiras – Airport – Portela / Prior Velho (work days only, with the operation alternating between Portela and Prior Velho. Night service, only to the Prior Velho);
- Marquês Pombal – Airport – Prior Velho (Saturday, Sunday and Holidays, with night service)

Price: 1,40€ + 0,50€ for Viva Viagem Electronic Card (rechargeable)
Average Journey Time: 40 minutes

SHUTTLE:

Working Hours:
LINE 1 - CITY CENTER
- Airport - Cais do Sodré: 7:00 am - 11:20 pm
- Cais do Sodré - Airport: 7:40 am - 11:00 pm
- Daily departures every 20 minutes
- Direct connection to both airport terminals (Terminal 1 and 2)

LINE 2 - FINANCIAL CENTER
- Airport - Av. José Malhoa Sul 7:30 am - 11:00 pm (daily)
- Daily departures every 40 minutes; from 8:00 pm every 60 minutes
- Av. José Malhoa Sul - Aeroporto 8:00 am - 11:30 pm (daily)
- Daily departures every 40 minutes; from 8:30 pm every 60 minutes
- Direct connection to both airport terminals (Terminal 1 and 2)
- Price: 3,50€
- Average Journey Time: 25 minutes

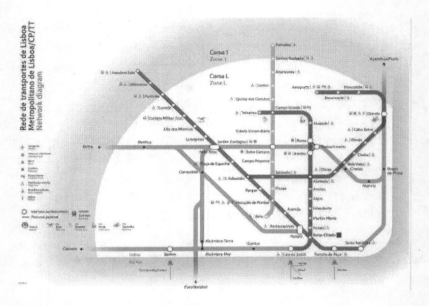

UBER (https://uberportugal.pt/):

Working Hours: Everyday| Price: Depends on the distance and time of the day

EMOV (https://emov.es/):

Emov is a new electric car rental service, where you download an app, give the necessary information and then you are able to look in the designated map where the service cars are, book one and unlock it and use it, only to leave it wherever you want (there a service limit in the city, from which you can get out of, but not park). You don't even need to pay for parking. Then you just lock the car and terminate the trip on your app, and you will receive an e-mail with the amount that will be debited from your account. All the cars are automatic.

Working Hours: Everyday| Price: 0,18€/min

eCOOLTRA (https://www.cooltra.com/pt/alugar-scooter-localizacao/aluger-motas-lisboa):

ecooltra is a scooter sharing service that works in the same way emov does. You only pay for the minutes you use, and it has the advantage of being possible to park it anywhere on the street.

Working Hours: Everyday| Price: 0,24€/min

GIRA (https://www.gira-bicicletasdelisboa.pt/):

Just like the previous means of transportation, Gira is a bicycle rental service, with classic and electric bicycles, that you can rent to move around the city. You have to leave these bicycles in their stations, which you can check out in the map in the app.

Working Hours: Everyday| Price: 2€/day

ZoomTip 1.2: Information on the Monuments
Santa Justa Lift

via Sandra Filipe Photography

Santa Justa Lift, also known as the Elevador de Santa Justa, is one of the most famous and iconic landmarks in Lisbon, Portugal. The lift, which is located in the heart of the city's historic district, connects the Baixa neighborhood to the Largo do Carmo square, providing visitors with stunning views of the city.

History of Santa Justa Lift

The Santa Justa Lift was built in the late 19th century as a way to connect the lower part of the city to the higher neighborhoods. The initial idea was to build a funicular, but it was later decided that an elevator would be a better solution. The lift was designed by Raoul Mesnier du Ponsard, a disciple of Gustave Eiffel, and it was inaugurated in 1902.

The lift was initially powered by steam, but it was later converted to electricity. It has since become a popular attraction for tourists and locals alike, offering incredible views of the city's rooftops and landmarks.

Design of Santa Justa Lift

One of the most striking features of the Santa Justa Lift is its beautiful design. The lift's iron structure is reminiscent of the Eiffel Tower in Paris, and it is often referred to as the "Eiffel Tower of Lisbon". The lift stands at a height of 45 meters (147 feet), and it is a perfect example of the Gothic Revival style that was popular in the late 19th century.

The lift is made up of two cages that can each hold up to 20 passengers. The cages are decorated with intricate woodwork, and they offer a comfortable ride to the top of the tower. The top of the lift provides visitors with breathtaking views of Lisbon, including the Rossio Square, the Castle of São Jorge, and the Tagus River.

Visiting Santa Justa Lift
The lift is located in the Baixa neighborhood, which is known for its vibrant atmosphere and historic landmarks. Visitors can reach the lift by foot or by taking one of the city's many trams or buses.

Once you arrive at the lift, you can purchase a ticket to ride to the top of the tower. The ticket includes access to a viewing platform that provides 360-degree views of Lisbon. Visitors can also take the stairs to the top of the tower, which provides a unique perspective of the lift's iron structure.

The lift is open daily from 7am to 11pm, and it can get quite crowded during peak tourist season. To avoid the crowds, it is recommended that visitors arrive early in the morning or later in the evening.

Nearby Attractions

The Santa Justa Lift is located in the heart of Lisbon's historic district, which is home to many other popular attractions. One of the most famous landmarks in the area is the **Rossio Square,** which is located just a short walk from the lift. The square is a popular meeting place for locals and tourists, and it is surrounded by cafes, restaurants, and shops.

Another popular attraction in the area is the **Castle of São Jorge**, which is located on a hill overlooking the city. The castle dates back to the 11th century, and it offers visitors incredible views of Lisbon and the Tagus River. The castle also has a museum and a restaurant on site.

If you're looking for something more cultural, the **Chiado Museum** is located just a short walk from the lift. The museum is dedicated to Portuguese art, and it features works by some of the country's most famous artists..

Opening Hours

June - September: 7:00 am to 10:45 pm, **October - May:** 7:00 am to 9:45 pm

Santa Justa Viewpoint: 8:30 am to 8:30 pm. Note: Closed on January 1st, May 1st, and December 25th | **Ticket Price**: 1,5€.

Commerce Square (commonly known as Terreiro do Paço)

via Sandra Filipe Photography

via Sandra Filipe Photography

Commerce Square, also known as Terreiro do Paço, is one of the most iconic and historic landmarks in Lisbon, Portugal. Located on the banks of the Tagus River, the square has played an important role in the city's history, and it remains a popular destination for tourists and locals alike.

History of Commerce Square

The square was originally built in the 16th century, during the reign of King Manuel I. The square was designed to be a grand entrance to the city, and it was the location of the royal palace until it was destroyed in the earthquake of 1755.

After the earthquake, the square was rebuilt, and it became the location of many government buildings, including the Ministry of Finance and the Post Office. It was also a popular gathering place for the city's residents, who would come to the square to shop, socialize, and watch public events.

In 2010, the square underwent a major renovation, which transformed it into a pedestrian-friendly area with shops, restaurants, and cafes. Today, the square remains a popular destination for visitors to Lisbon, offering a mix of historic landmarks and modern amenities.

Design of Commerce Square

One of the most striking features of Commerce Square is its grandeur. The square is 36,000 square meters (387,500 square feet) in size, and it is surrounded by impressive buildings that date back to the 18th and 19th centuries.

The centerpiece of the square is the Arco da Rua Augusta, a triumphal arch that was completed in 1873. The arch is decorated with statues and reliefs that represent the city's history, including its patron saint, St. George.

The square is also home to a statue of King Joseph I, who ruled Portugal in the mid-18th century. The statue is surrounded by water fountains, which add to the grandeur of the square.

Visiting Commerce Square

The square is located in the **Baixa neighborhood,** which is known for its vibrant atmosphere and historic landmarks. Visitors can reach the square by foot or by taking one of the city's many trams or buses.

Once you arrive at the square, you can take a leisurely stroll around the area, admiring the grandeur of the buildings and the impressive architecture. You can also take a closer look at the **Arco da Rua Augusta**, which is one of the most famous landmarks in Lisbon.

If you're looking for something to do, the square is surrounded by shops, restaurants, and cafes. You can spend an afternoon browsing the shops, sampling traditional Portuguese cuisine, or simply relaxing with a cup of coffee.

Nearby Attractions

Commerce Square is located in the heart of **Lisbon's historic district**, which is home to many other popular attractions. One of the most famous landmarks in the area is the **Santa Justa Lift**, which is located just a short walk from the square. The lift offers visitors incredible views of Lisbon, and it is a must-do for anyone visiting the city.

Another popular attraction in the area is the **Castle of São Jorge**, which is located on a hill overlooking the city. The castle dates back to the 11th century, and it offers visitors incredible views of Lisbon and the Tagus River. The castle also has a museum and a restaurant on site.

If you're looking for something more cultural, the **Chiado Museum** is located just a short walk from the square. The museum is dedicated to Portuguese art, and it features works by some of the country's most famous artists.

St. George's Castle

via Sandra Filipe Photography

Located in one of Lisbon's hills, this 11th-century castle was initially constructed by the Muslims to protect the population who lived inside its walls. However, the Muslims did not realize that the fortress would be unable to resist D. Afonso Henriques and its army in 1147, the remarkable date when the first King of Portugal conquered Lisbon. Since then, the castle became a royal house, becoming one of the most important places in Portugal to receive the king and his entire royal court.

Opening Hours: March - October: - 9:00 am to 9:00 pm (last entrance at 8:30 pm), November - February: - 9:00 am to 6:00 pm (last entry at 5:30 pm), Note: Closed on January 1st, December 24th, 25th, and 31st.
Ticket Price: 8,5€ (Students < 25 years old: 5€)

Lisbon Cathedral (commonly known as Sé de Lisboa)

via Câmara Municipal de Lisboa

Lisbon Cathedral, commonly known as Sé de Lisboa, is one of the oldest and most significant landmarks in Lisbon, Portugal. The cathedral, which dates back to the 12th century, is an important piece of Lisbon's history and a must-see for anyone visiting the city.

History of Lisbon Cathedral
Lisbon Cathedral was originally built in the 12th century, during the reign of King Afonso Henriques. The cathedral was built on the site of a former

mosque, which was destroyed when the city was conquered by the Christian forces.

Over the years, the cathedral has undergone many changes and renovations, but it has remained an important piece of Lisbon's history. It was the location of many important events, including the baptism of Prince Henry the Navigator in the 15th century.

Design of Lisbon Cathedral

Lisbon Cathedral is an impressive example of Romanesque architecture, with a mix of Gothic and Baroque influences. The cathedral is made up of several chapels, including the Chapel of St. Vincent and the Chapel of Our Lady of Guadalupe.

One of the most striking features of the cathedral is its bell tower, which stands at a height of 80 meters (262 feet). The tower is a popular destination for visitors, offering stunning views of Lisbon and the Tagus River.

Inside the cathedral, visitors can admire the impressive nave, which is decorated with beautiful stained glass windows and intricate carvings. The cathedral is also home to a museum, which contains many important artifacts from Lisbon's history.

Visiting Lisbon Cathedral

Visiting Lisbon Cathedral is a must-do for anyone interested in history or architecture. The cathedral is located in the Alfama neighborhood, which is known for its charming atmosphere and narrow streets.

Visitors can reach the cathedral by foot or by taking one of the city's many trams or buses. Once you arrive, you can take a guided tour of the cathedral, which will provide you with a deeper understanding of its history and significance.

If you're interested in the tower, you can purchase a ticket to climb to the top. The climb can be quite steep, but the views from the top are well worth the effort.

Opening Hours: Monday - Saturday: 9:00 am to 7:00 pm | Sunday: 9:00 am to 8:00 pm | **Ticket Price**: Free

ZoomTip 1.3: Time Out Mercado da Ribeira

via Sandra Filipe Photography

Located in the same location where once stood one of the oldest (1982), most important and largest food markets in Lisbon, ***Ribeira's Market***, Time Out Mercado da Ribeira is a place you would like to visit and, therefore, experience its culinary diversity. Time Out Lisboa, a well-known tourist magazine, took over the old market's management and completely transformed it in a modern, contemporary and up-to-the-minute food & drink large stall, housing various restaurants from renowned chefs. The atmosphere is unique and captivating, so you will probably don't want to leave this place after the moment you stepped on it.

Price: 7€ - ?€ (Depends on the food and drink stalls you choose)

Time Out Mercado da Ribeira

Avenida 24 de Julho, 50| 1200-481 Lisbon| Tel: (00351) 21 346 2966 |

Official Website: http://www.timeout.com/city-guides/time-out-mercado-da-ribeira-lisbon

Tip #1: *To get to Belém, you have two options:*

a. Take the metro from *Anjos* (Green Line – Direction: Cais do Sodré) just outside your hotel, exit at *Martim Moniz* and walk to *Praça da Figueira*. However, since it is only a 15 minute (1.4 km) walk from your hotel to *Praça da Figueira*, it will probably be faster on foot. Then, catch the Tram #15 in *Praça da Figueira* to *Belém* (25 minutes).

b. Take the metro from *Anjos* (Green Line – Direction: Cais do Sodré) and leave at the last station: *Cais do Sodré*. Then catch the train to *Belém*. However, due to the fact of *Cais do Sodré* station is located nearby the cruise port if a cruise arrives there will be lots (actually, lots!) of tourists waiting for the same train as you. Given that fact, we highly recommend you follow the steps presented in Option 1.

c. Emov – within the area of service

Tip #2: All the attractions are close, within a short walking distance from each other in one of the most beautiful areas in Lisbon – Belém!

10:00

Visit the Jerónimos Monastery (Mosteiro dos Jerónimos)

View *ZoomTip 2.1* | **Ticket Price**: 10€ (Students: 5€)

11:30

Eat Lisbon's most iconic pastry called *nata*, in *Pastéis de Belém*.

View *ZoomTip 2.2* | **Price:** approx. 2,5€ (*nata* + expresso)

12:00

Visit the Belém Tower (Torre de Belém), while passing by the Monument to the Discoveries (Padrão dos Descobrimentos)

View *ZoomTip 2.1* | **Ticket Price**: 6€ (Students: 3€)

13:45

Lunch at *Enoteca de Belém*

If you're looking for a top-notch dining experience in Lisbon, look no further than Enoteca de Belém. This renowned restaurant, located just across the street, offers an impressive and extensive wine list, pairing it with expertly prepared dishes that fuse traditional Portuguese cuisine with modern cooking techniques.

Enoteca de Belém's elegant and inviting atmosphere is the perfect setting for a leisurely lunch, where you can savor each dish and sip on a glass of carefully selected wine. Their menu features a range of options, from seafood to meat dishes, all expertly prepared with fresh, locally sourced ingredients.

Whether you're a wine connoisseur or simply enjoy a good glass of wine, Enoteca de Belém is a must-visit for its exceptional wine selection. The knowledgeable and friendly staff are always happy to make recommendations and guide you through the wine list to find the perfect pairing for your meal.

So, if you're looking for a memorable dining experience in Lisbon, head over to Enoteca de Belém for a taste of some of the city's finest cuisine and wine.

Price: Depends on what you choose (<u>Average</u>: 15€ - 20€ per person)

16:00

Visit the Cultural Centre of Belém, also known as CCB, with a particular focus on the Berardo Collection Museum *(Museu Coleção Berardo)*

View *ZoomTip 2.1* | **Ticket Price**: 3€

18:00

Enjoy a refreshing Ice Cream at Nosolo Italia

After a long day exploring the sunny streets of Lisbon, there's nothing quite like a refreshing ice cream to cool off. Lucky for you, there's a fantastic Italian-style gelateria just a stone's throw away. At Nosolo Italia, you can relax and indulge in a variety of delicious and unique ice cream flavors.

With its cozy atmosphere and friendly staff, Nosolo Italia is the perfect place to take a break and enjoy a sweet treat. Their menu features a range of flavors, from classic options like vanilla and chocolate to more exotic choices like passion fruit and tiramisu.

Price: Depending on what you choose, but it should be between 3€ - 5€.

20:00

Dinner at the *Bairro Alto* area, Lisbon's nightlife heart
Address: Rua das Gáveas 69/71, Lisbon, Tel: 21 346 8557

When in Lisbon, a visit to the Bairro Alto neighborhood is a must, especially for those seeking a vibrant and exciting nightlife scene. While there are many restaurants and bars in the area, we highly recommend dining at "Lisboa à Noite" for an unforgettable dinner experience.

Located at Rua das Gáveas 69/71 and easily accessible by public transport or taxi, Lisboa à Noite has been a landmark in Bairro Alto for over a decade. The restaurant boasts a traditional atmosphere, with arched rooms that transport you back to 19th century Lisbon, making for a unique and memorable dining experience.

But what sets Lisboa à Noite apart is the incredible food. The menu features a variety of traditional Portuguese dishes, prepared with locally sourced ingredients, and cooked to perfection. From seafood to meat dishes, there is something for everyone to enjoy.

Pair your meal with a glass of Portuguese wine or a refreshing cocktail and soak up the lively atmosphere of the Bairro Alto district. With its prime location and exceptional food, Lisboa à Noite is a must-visit for anyone looking to experience the best of Lisbon's dining scene.

Price: 10€ - 15€

Admire Lisbon's beautiful historic skyline through a rooftop bar.

After a long day of exploring Lisbon, you may be feeling exhausted, but don't let that stop you from making the most of your last night in the city. What better way to end your trip than by relaxing on a rooftop bar, sipping a gin & tonic or a cocktail while taking in the stunning skyline of Portugal's capital city? Just a short distance from the restaurant where you enjoyed dinner, you'll find the **BA Terrace,** the rooftop terrace bar and restaurant of the luxurious 5-star Bairro Alto Hotel.

Considered the 4th best hotel-terrace view in the world, the BA Terrace is the perfect place to take in the breathtaking view of the Tagus River and the 25th of April Bridge at night. The twinkling city lights create a unique and memorable atmosphere for your last evening in Lisbon.

The opening hours for this establishment vary depending on the season. During the winter, the hours are from 10:30 am to 10:00 pm on Sunday through Thursday and from 10:30 am to 1:00 am on Fridays and Saturdays. In the summer, the establishment is open from 10:30 am to 1:00 am every day.

2nd Day in Lisbon Map

Get the below google maps at https://bit.ly/lisbondaytwo

ZoomTip 2.1: Information on the Monuments

Jerónimos Monastery

via Sandra Filipe Photography

Jerónimos Monastery, also known as Mosteiro dos Jerónimos, is a UNESCO World Heritage Site and one of the most famous landmarks in Lisbon, Portugal. The monastery, which dates back to the 16th century, is an important piece of Portuguese history and a must-see for anyone visiting the city.

History of Jerónimos Monastery

Jerónimos Monastery was built in the early 16th century, during the reign of King Manuel I. The monastery was built to commemorate Vasco da Gama's successful voyage to India, which brought great wealth and prosperity to Portugal.

Over the years, the monastery has undergone many changes and renovations, but it has remained an important piece of Portuguese history. It was the location of many important events, including the baptism of King Manuel I's son in the 16th century.

Design of Jerónimos Monastery
Jerónimos Monastery is an impressive example of Manueline architecture, with a mix of Gothic and Renaissance influences. The monastery is made up of several chapels, including the Chapel of St. Jerome and the Chapel of Our Lady of Belém.

One of the most striking features of the monastery is its cloisters, which are decorated with beautiful stone carvings and intricate details. The cloisters are a popular destination for visitors, offering a tranquil and peaceful atmosphere.

Inside the monastery, visitors can admire the impressive nave, which is decorated with beautiful stained glass windows and intricate carvings. The monastery is also home to a museum, which contains many important artifacts from Portugal's history.

Visiting Jerónimos Monastery
Visiting Jerónimos Monastery is a must-do for anyone interested in history or architecture. The monastery is located in the Belém neighborhood, which is known for its charming atmosphere and beautiful gardens.

Visitors can reach the monastery by foot or by taking one of the city's many trams or buses. Once you arrive, you can take a guided tour of the monastery, which will provide you with a deeper understanding of its history and significance.

If you're interested in the cloisters, you can spend some time walking around and admiring the intricate details. The cloisters are a peaceful and tranquil space, and they offer a respite from the bustling city outside.

Nearby Attractions

Jerónimos Monastery is located in the heart of the Belém neighborhood, which is home to many other popular attractions. One of the most famous landmarks in the area is the **Belém Tower**, which is located on the banks of the Tagus River. The tower dates back to the 16th century, and it is a must-see for anyone visiting Lisbon.

Another popular attraction in the area is the **Padrão dos Descobrimentos,** a monument that celebrates Portugal's Age of Discovery. The monument is located on the banks of the Tagus River, and it offers stunning views of Lisbon.

If you're looking for something more cultural, the **Belém Cultural Center** is located just a short walk from the monastery. The center is home to a range of cultural events and exhibitions, including music concerts, theater performances, and art shows.

Opening Hours: Tuesday to Sunday: 10am to 5pm| Closed on Mondays, January 1st, Easter Sunday, May 1st and December 25th.

Entry Ticket Prices: Adults: €12.00(Students: 5€). We recommend you to buy a combined ticket of Jerónimos Monastery and Belém Tower for 12€.

Monument to the Discoveries

The Monument to the Discoveries, or Padrão dos Descobrimentos in Portuguese, is a famous monument in Lisbon, Portugal that celebrates Portugal's Age of Discovery. The monument, which was erected in 1960, is an impressive work of art that offers visitors a unique perspective on the country's rich history.

History of Monument to the Discoveries

The Monument to the Discoveries was built in 1960 to commemorate the 500th anniversary of the death of Prince Henry the Navigator, a famous Portuguese explorer who played a significant role in the Age of Discovery.

The monument was designed by architect Cottinelli Telmo and sculptor Leopoldo de Almeida, and it features a range of famous historical figures, including Vasco da Gama, Ferdinand Magellan, and many others.

Design of Monument to the Discoveries

The Monument to the Discoveries is an impressive work of art that stands at a height of 52 meters (171 feet). The monument is shaped like a caravel, a type of ship that was commonly used during the Age of Discovery, and it features a range of famous historical figures.

One of the most striking features of the monument is its large compass rose, which is made up of stone and mosaic tiles. The compass rose is a nod to Portugal's long history of navigation and exploration.

Visiting Monument to the Discoveries

Visiting the Monument to the Discoveries is a must-do for anyone interested in history or art. The monument is located on the banks of the Tagus River, and it offers stunning views of Lisbon and the surrounding area.

Visitors can reach the monument by foot or by taking one of the city's many trams or buses. Once you arrive, you can spend some time admiring the impressive sculpture and the views from the top of the monument.

If you're interested in learning more about Portugal's history, you can visit the nearby **Maritime Museum**, which is dedicated to the country's long history of navigation and exploration.

Opening Hours: Tuesday to Sunday: 10am to 6pm| Closed on Mondays, January 1st, Easter Sunday, May 1st and December 25th.

Entry Ticket Prices: Adults: €6.00| Children under 12: Free| Seniors and Students: €3.00

Belém Tower

via Sandra Filipe Photography

Belém Tower, also known as Torre de Belém in Portuguese, is one of the most famous landmarks in Lisbon, Portugal. The tower, which dates back to the 16th century, is an important piece of Portuguese history and a must-see for anyone visiting the city.

History of Belém Tower

Belém Tower was built in the early 16th century, during the reign of King Manuel I. The tower was built to defend the Tagus River and the city of Lisbon from invaders.

Over the years, the tower has undergone many changes and renovations, but it has remained an important piece of Portuguese history. It was the location of many important events, including the departure of Vasco da Gama on his voyage to India in the 15th century.

Design of Belém Tower

Belém Tower is an impressive example of Manueline architecture, which is a unique style of architecture that was developed in Portugal during the 16th century. The tower is made up of several levels, including a watchtower and a fortified bastion.

One of the most striking features of the tower is its intricate carvings, which include depictions of maritime motifs, animals, and saints. The tower is also decorated with beautiful stone filigree work and other intricate details.

Visiting Belém Tower

Visiting Belém Tower is a must-do for anyone interested in history or architecture. The tower is located on the banks of the Tagus River, and it offers stunning views of Lisbon and the surrounding area.

If you're interested in the tower's defensive features, you can spend some time exploring the various levels and admiring the intricate carvings and other details.

Opening Hours: Tuesday to Sunday: 10am to 5pm| Closed on Mondays, January 1st, Easter Sunday, May 1st and December 25th.

Entry Ticket Prices: Adults: €6.00| Children under 12: Free| Seniors and Students: €3.00

Berardo Collection Museum

via Sandra Filipe Photography

via Sandra Filipe Photography

The Berardo Collection Museum is a modern and contemporary art museum located in Lisbon, Portugal. The museum is home to an impressive collection of artworks from the 20th and 21st centuries, and it is a must-visit for anyone interested in modern art.

History of Berardo Collection Museum

The Berardo Collection Museum was founded in 2007 by the Portuguese businessman and art collector Joe Berardo. Berardo began collecting art in the 1960s, and his collection has grown to include over 1,000 artworks from some of the most famous artists of the 20th and 21st centuries.

Design of Berardo Collection Museum

The Berardo Collection Museum is located in the Belém Cultural Center, which was designed by the Portuguese architect Vittorio Gregotti. The museum is spread over two floors, and it features a range of different exhibition spaces, including galleries, corridors, and open areas.

The museum's permanent collection is divided into several different themes, including surrealism, pop art, and abstract expressionism. The museum also hosts temporary exhibitions throughout the year, which feature works from both established and emerging artists.

Top 10 Exhibits to See at Berardo Collection Museum
- Salvador Dalí - The museum is home to a range of works by Salvador Dalí, including his famous painting "The Persistence of Memory." Visitors can also see some of Dalí's sculptures and other works of art.
- Andy Warhol - The museum has an impressive collection of works by Andy Warhol, including some of his famous "soup can" paintings.
- Pablo Picasso - The museum has several works by Pablo Picasso, including some of his famous cubist paintings.
- Joan Miró - The museum has an extensive collection of works by Joan Miró, including some of his famous surrealist paintings.
- Jackson Pollock - The museum has several works by Jackson Pollock, including his famous "drip paintings."
- Roy Lichtenstein - The museum has several works by Roy Lichtenstein, including some of his famous comic book-style paintings.
- Jeff Koons - The museum has several works by Jeff Koons, including his famous sculpture "Balloon Dog."
- Francis Bacon - The museum has several works by Francis Bacon, including some of his famous distorted portraits.
- Gerhard Richter - The museum has several works by Gerhard Richter, including some of his famous abstract paintings.
- Yves Klein - The museum has several works by Yves Klein, including some of his famous monochromatic blue paintings.

The Berardo Collection Museum is a must-visit for anyone interested in modern and contemporary art. The museum's impressive collection of works by some of the most famous artists of the 20th and 21st centuries make it one of the most important art museums in Portugal.

Opening Hours: Monday: 10am to 6pm| Tuesday to Sunday: 10am to 7pm
Entry Ticket Prices: Adults: €5.00| Seniors, Students and Youth (13-18): €3.50| Children under 12: Free

ZoomTip 2.2: Pastéis de Belém

via Sandra Filipe Photography

Pastéis de Belém is a famous pastry shop located in the Belém neighborhood of Lisbon, Portugal. The pastry shop is renowned for its pastel de nata, a traditional Portuguese custard tart that is famous around the world.

History of Pastéis de Belém

Pastéis de Belém has been in business since 1837, and it has become a must-visit destination for anyone visiting Lisbon. The pastry shop was originally located in the same building as the Jerónimos Monastery, and it quickly became popular among the monks and the local community.

Over the years, Pastéis de Belém has become a famous landmark in Lisbon, attracting visitors from all over the world who come to taste the shop's famous pastel de nata.

The Pastel de Nata

The pastel de nata is a traditional Portuguese pastry that is made with puff pastry and a custard filling. The pastry is typically dusted with cinnamon and powdered sugar, and it is best served warm.

Pastéis de Belém is renowned for its pastel de nata, which is made according to a secret recipe that has been passed down through the generations. The pastry shop sells over 20,000 pastéis de nata every day, and visitors can watch as the pastries are made in the open kitchen.

The pastry shop is located in the heart of the Belém neighborhood, and it is easily accessible by tram or bus. Once you arrive, you can join the queue to order your pastel de nata. The pastry shop is always busy, so it's best to arrive early in the day to avoid the crowds. If you're not in the mood for a pastel de nata, you can also try some of the shop's other delicious pastries, including croissants, quiches, and other sweet treats.

Price: approx. 2,50€ (*nata* + expresso)

Pastéis de Belém| Official Website / Facebook| Opening Hours: Everyday from 8:00am to 11:00pm

Indicative Prices: Pastel de Nata: €1.10 per unit| Espresso: €0.70|

Cappuccino: €1.10| Croissant: €1.10| Quiche: €2.60

Tip #1: *How to get from your hotel to the National Museum of Ancient Art:*

Take the metro from *Anjos* (Green Line – Direction: Cais do Sodré) and leave at the last station: *Cais do Sodré*. Then, take the bus 706 and go at *Largo Vitorino Damásio* (3 stops from *Cais do Sodré*). The National Museum of Ancient Art is just near, at an 800m short walk.

Tip #2: *How to get from the National Museum of Ancient Art to the Park of Nations:*

To make your way from the National Museum of Ancient Art to the Park of Nations, simply retrace your steps back to the Cais do Sodré metro station. Once there, take the Green Line subway in the direction of Telheiras, and exit at the Alameda station. From there, transfer to the Red Line platform, traveling towards Airport/Aeroporto, and disembark at Oriente, located in the heart of the Park of Nations.

Oriente Station is the largest station in Lisbon, serving a variety of metro, train, and international bus companies. Designed by the renowned architect Santiago Calatrava, the station is a work of art in itself and is also connected to the Vasco da Gama Shopping Center.

Navigating the Lisbon metro system is an easy and efficient way to get around the city, and Oriente Station is a hub for multiple lines, making it a convenient starting point for exploring the Park of Nations and other popular destinations. With this helpful tip, you'll be on your way in no time.

10:00

Visit the National Museum of Ancient Art

View *ZoomTip 3.1* | **Ticket Price**: 6€ (Students: 3€)

12:30

Lunch at *"Honorato"* Restaurant

View *ZoomTip 3.2* | **Price:** 8€ - 12,5€ per person

14:00

Visit the *Lisbon Oceanarium (Oceanário de Lisboa)*

View *ZoomTip 3.1* | Ticket Price: 15.3€ per person

16:00

Visit the *Pavillion of Knowledge (Pavilhão do Conhecimento – Ciência Viva)*

View *ZoomTip 3.1* | **Ticket Price:** 8€ (Students: 4€)

18:30

Photograph the *Pavillion of Portugal* (Pavilhão de Portugal) and MEO Arena (ex – Atlantic Pavillion)

View *ZoomTip 3.1*

19:00

Enjoy the *Cable Car Ride* from Oceanarium to Vasco da Gama Tower

View *ZoomTip 3.1* | **Ticket Price**: 3,95€ (One-way) / 5,90€ (Return)

19:15

Admire and Photograph *Vasco da Gama Tower*

View *ZoomTip 3.1*

20:00

Return to *Origami Lisbon Hostel (or other hotel of your choice)*

Return to your hotel, refresh and get some rest before dinner.

Dinner at "Portugália Cervejaria"

Portugália Cervejaria is a popular Lisbon restaurant that offers a range of traditional Portuguese cuisine and beer. The restaurant has been a local favorite for over 90 years, and it's no surprise why.

If you're looking to try some of the best Portuguese dishes, Portugália Cervejaria is the perfect place to go. One of the most popular dishes is the **steak sandwich**, made with tender beef and served on a fresh roll. Another must-try is the **grilled prawns**, which are cooked to perfection and bursting with flavor.

In addition to these classic dishes, be sure to try two other Portuguese staples: **codfish and mussels**. Portugália Cervejaria serves some of the best codfish in Lisbon, with a variety of preparations available, from grilled to baked. And for the seafood lover, the mussels are not to be missed, cooked in a delicious white wine and garlic sauce.

To finish off your meal, don't forget to indulge in one of the restaurant's famous desserts, such as the **crème brûlée.**

If you plan to visit, be sure to make a reservation in advance to avoid any wait time. The restaurant also offers a bar area where you can relax and enjoy a cold beer or cocktail before your meal.

Tips: Get a seat next to the window for some people-watching. It is not a cheap restaurant; however, it is good value for money. The best price options are given at the desk "balcão".

Price: around 25€ per person | **Address:** Av. Alm. Reis 117, 1150-014 Lisboa, tel +351 21 314 0002

Return to the Hotel

3rd Day in Lisbon Map

Get this map at https://bit.ly/lisbondaythree

Zoom Tip 3.1 – Information on the Attractions

National Museum of Ancient Art

The National Museum of Ancient Art (Museu Nacional de Arte Antiga) is located in the city of Lisbon, Portugal, and is one of the most important art museums in the country. The museum is housed in a beautiful 17th-century palace, and it is home to a vast collection of European art from the 12th to the 19th century.

History of the National Museum of Ancient Art

The National Museum of Ancient Art was founded in 1884 by the Portuguese government, and it was originally housed in the Palácio de São Francisco in Lisbon. The museum was later moved to its current location in the Palácio das Janelas Verdes in 1902, where it has remained ever since.

The museum has gone through several renovations and expansions over the years, but its collection of European art has remained its primary focus. Today, the museum is a must-visit for anyone interested in art and history.

Top Exhibits to See

The National Museum of Ancient Art has a vast collection of art, and it can be overwhelming to try to see everything. Here are some of the top exhibits to see at the museum:

The Namban Screens - These six-panel screens were created in Japan in the 16th century and depict Portuguese traders and Jesuit missionaries in Japan.

The Temptation of St. Anthony - This painting by the Flemish artist Hieronymus Bosch is one of the most important works in the museum's collection. It depicts the temptations of St. Anthony and is full of fantastical creatures and surreal images.

The Portuguese Tableware - The museum has an impressive collection of Portuguese tableware from the 15th to the 18th century. The collection includes pieces made from porcelain, faience, and silver, and it provides a glimpse into the history of Portuguese dining and entertaining.

The Polyptych of St. Vincent - This beautiful polyptych was created by the Portuguese painter Nuno Gonçalves in the 15th century. The painting depicts St. Vincent, the patron saint of Lisbon, and is an important example of Portuguese Renaissance art.

The Flemish Tapestries - The museum has a collection of Flemish tapestries from the 15th and 16th centuries. These tapestries are notable for their intricate designs and beautiful colors.

Address: R. das Janelas Verdes, 1249-017 Lisboa, Portugal

Opening Hours: Tuesday to Sunday: 10:00am to 6:00pm| Closed on Mondays, as well as January 1st, Easter Sunday, May 1st, and December 25th

Ticket Prices: General Admission: €6.00| Students and Seniors: €3.00| Children under 12: Free

Lisbon Oceanarium

via Sandra Filipe Photography

The Lisbon Oceanarium, located in the Parque das Nações neighborhood of Lisbon, Portugal, is the largest indoor aquarium in Europe and one of the city's most popular tourist attractions. The oceanarium is home to a vast array of marine life from all over the world, including sharks, rays, octopuses, and penguins.

The Lisbon Oceanarium was designed by the American architect Peter Chermayeff and was built as part of the Expo '98 World's Fair. The oceanarium opened its doors to the public in 1998, and it quickly became one of the most popular attractions at the fair.

Today, the Lisbon Oceanarium is one of the most visited tourist attractions in Lisbon, and it is considered to be one of the best aquariums in the world.

Top Exhibits to See

The Lisbon Oceanarium is home to a vast array of marine life, and it can be overwhelming to try to see everything. Here are some of the top exhibits to see at the oceanarium:

The Main Tank - This enormous tank is the heart of the oceanarium and is home to a variety of marine life, including sharks, rays, and tuna. Visitors can walk through a transparent tunnel that runs through the center of the tank, providing a unique view of the marine life.

The Sea Otters - The Lisbon Oceanarium is home to a group of sea otters, which are known for their playful and curious nature. Visitors can watch as the otters swim, play, and interact with each other.

The Penguins - The oceanarium has a large colony of penguins, which are always a crowd favorite. Visitors can watch as the penguins swim, dive, and play on the rocky shores of their exhibit.

The Octopus - The Lisbon Oceanarium is home to several species of octopus, including the giant Pacific octopus. Visitors can watch as the octopuses move and change color, demonstrating their incredible intelligence and adaptability.

The Coral Reef - The oceanarium has a stunning exhibit dedicated to the world's coral reefs. Visitors can see a variety of colorful fish and other marine life that call the reefs their home.

Address: Esplanada D. Carlos I s/nº, 1990-005 Lisboa, Portugal

Opening Hours: October to May: 10:00am to 6:00pm | June to September: 10:00am to 7:00pm

Ticket Prices: General Admission: €19.00 | Children (0-3 years old): Free | Children (4-12 years old): €13.00 | Students and Seniors: €14.50

Pavillion of Knowledge

via Portal das Nações

The Pavillion of Knowledge (Pavilhão do Conhecimento) is a science and technology museum located in the Parque das Nações neighborhood of Lisbon, Portugal. The museum is housed in a modern building and is home to a variety of interactive exhibits and activities that are designed to educate and entertain visitors of all ages.

The Pavillion of Knowledge was built as part of the Expo '98 World's Fair, which was held in Lisbon. The museum was designed to be a place where visitors could learn about science and technology in a fun and interactive way.

Today, the Pavillion of Knowledge is one of the most popular science museums in Portugal, and it is considered to be a must-visit destination for anyone interested in science and technology.

Top Exhibits to See
- The Pavillion of Knowledge is home to a variety of exhibits and activities that are designed to educate and entertain visitors. Here are some of the top exhibits to see at the museum:
- The Human Body Exhibit - This exhibit explores the human body and how it works. Visitors can learn about the different systems in the

body, including the circulatory system, the respiratory system, and the digestive system.

- The Planetarium - The Pavillion of Knowledge has a state-of-the-art planetarium that offers visitors a unique view of the universe. Visitors can watch as the stars and planets move across the dome, and learn about the mysteries of the cosmos.
- The Energy Exhibit - This exhibit explores the different forms of energy and how they are used in our daily lives. Visitors can learn about renewable energy, such as solar and wind power, and see how it is changing the world.
- The Mind Exhibit - This exhibit explores the mysteries of the human mind and how it works. Visitors can learn about the different parts of the brain and how they control our thoughts, emotions, and actions.
- The Water Exhibit - This exhibit explores the importance of water and its role in the environment. Visitors can learn about the water cycle, water conservation, and the different ways that water is used around the world.

Address: Largo José Mariano Gago 1, 1990-223 Lisboa, Portugal

Opening Hours: Tuesday to Friday: 10:00am to 6:00pm|Saturday, Sunday, and Public Holidays: 11:00am to 7:00pm| Closed on Mondays, as well as December 24th and 25th|

Ticket Prices: General Admission: €9.00| Children (3-11 years old): €6.00 Students and Seniors: €6.50| Family Ticket (2 adults + 2 children): €24.00

Pavillion of Portugal & MEO Arena

These two gigantic structures cannot but be noticed by everyone walking around their area. Like all the main buildings in this area, both structures were constructed during the EXPO 98 era with the purpose to house the country's national exposition (Pavillion of Portugal), as well as for the great night show (Atlantic Pavillion). The last one changed its name to MEO Arena a few years ago, becoming the biggest venue in Portugal for sports, music or any other kind of show.

Note: Not opened to the public, unless if it is running a temporal exposition.

Lisbon Cable Car

via Sandra Filipe Photography

The Lisbon Cable Car (Teleférico de Lisboa) is a cable car system that offers visitors a unique view of the city of Lisbon. The cable car runs from the Parque das Nações neighborhood to the Vasco da Gama Tower, providing breathtaking views of the Tagus River and the city skyline.

The Lisbon Cable Car was built as part of the Expo '98 World's Fair, which was held in Lisbon. The cable car was designed to provide visitors with a unique way to experience the fair, and it quickly became one of the most popular attractions at the event.

Today, the Lisbon Cable Car is one of the most popular tourist attractions in Lisbon, and it is considered to be a must-see destination for anyone visiting the city.

Address: Alameda dos Oceanos, 1990-223 Lisboa, Portugal

Opening Hours: Monday to Friday: 11:00am to 7:00pm| Saturday, Sunday, and Public Holidays: 10:00am to 7:00pm|

Ticket Prices: Single Ticket (One Way): €6.00| Round Trip Ticket: €10.00| Children under 6: Free

Note: The cable car closes due to maintenance reasons from 9th to 27th November.

Vasco da Gama Tower

via Sandra Filipe Photography

The Vasco da Gama Tower (Torre Vasco da Gama) is a modern tower located in the Parque das Nações neighborhood of Lisbon, Portugal. The tower is one of the tallest buildings in the city, and it offers visitors stunning views of the surrounding area.

The Vasco da Gama Tower was built as part of the Expo '98 World's Fair, which was held in Lisbon. The tower was designed to be a symbol of the fair, and it was named after the famous Portuguese explorer Vasco da Gama.

Today, the Vasco da Gama Tower is one of the most popular tourist attractions in Lisbon, and it is considered to be a must-see destination for anyone visiting the city.

Top Features of the Vasco da Gama Tower

- The Vasco da Gama Tower is a unique and modern tower that offers visitors a variety of features and amenities. Here are some of the top features of the tower
- Breathtaking Views - The Vasco da Gama Tower offers visitors stunning views of the Tagus River and the surrounding area. Visitors can take an elevator to the top of the tower, where they can enjoy panoramic views of the city.
- Restaurant - The Vasco da Gama Tower is home to a gourmet restaurant, which offers visitors a unique and unforgettable dining

experience. The restaurant serves a variety of Portuguese and international dishes, and it offers stunning views of the city.

- Sky Bar - The tower's Sky Bar offers visitors a selection of cocktails and other drinks, as well as a comfortable and relaxed atmosphere. The bar is located on the 16th floor of the tower, and it offers stunning views of the city.
- Observation Deck - The tower's observation deck offers visitors a unique and unforgettable experience. Visitors can take an elevator to the top of the tower, where they can enjoy panoramic views of the city from a height of over 100 meters.

Address: Av. Dom João II, 1990-095 Lisboa, Portugal

Opening Hours: Sunday to Thursday: 10:00am to 10:00pm| Friday and Saturday: 10:00am to 11:00pm

Ticket Prices: Observation Deck: €5.00| Observation Deck + Sky Bar: €7.50| Observation Deck + Gourmet Restaurant: Prices vary depending on the menu

Zoom Tip 3.2 – Honorato

via Sandra Filipe Photography

Honorato is a popular burger restaurant chain located in Lisbon, Portugal. With several locations throughout the city, Honorato is known for its delicious and high-quality burgers, as well as its friendly and welcoming atmosphere.

Honorato was founded in 2007 by a group of friends who shared a passion for good food and great company. The founders were inspired by their travels around the world, where they discovered a love for high-quality burgers and the community that often surrounded them. Today,

Honorato is one of the most popular burger chains in Lisbon, and it is considered to be a must-visit destination for anyone looking for delicious and high-quality burgers.

Honorato has several locations throughout Lisbon, making it easy to find a restaurant no matter where you are in the city. Here are some of the most popular locations:

Honorato Chiado - Rua do Alecrim, 24, 1200-014 Lisboa, Portugal

Honorato Amoreiras - Centro Comercial Amoreiras, Rua Professor Carlos de Rêsende, 1070-051 Lisboa, Portugal

Honorato Colombo - Centro Comercial Colombo, Av. Lusíada, 1500-392 Lisboa, Portugal

Honorato Alameda dos Oceanos, 2, 11 – 01, Fraction H/I, 1990-225 Lisbon

Tel: (00351) 93 256 1524, Official Website / Facebook

Opening Hours: Monday to Sunday: 12:00pm to 12:00am

Price: 8€ - 12,5€ per person

Thank You!

As we come to the end of our travel guide to Lisbon, we hope you have found it informative and useful in planning your visit to this beautiful city. From the stunning architecture and historical landmarks, to the delicious cuisine and exciting nightlife, there is truly something for everyone in Lisbon. We encourage you to explore beyond the main tourist areas and discover the hidden gems and unique experiences that make Lisbon so special.

Remember to take advantage of the local transportation options and plan your itinerary ahead of time to make the most of your trip. We also encourage you to be a responsible traveler and respect the local culture and environment.

Thank you for using our travel guide and we wish you a wonderful and unforgettable trip to Lisbon.

Your friends at Guidora.

Copyright Notice

Guidora Lisbon in 3 Days Travel Guide ©

Disclaimer

The publishers have checked the information in this travel guide, but its accuracy is not warranted or guaranteed. Tokyo visitors are advised that opening times should always be checked before making a journey.

Tracing Copyright Owners

Every effort has been done to trace the copyright holders of referred material. Where these efforts have not been successful, copyright owners are invited to contact the Editor (Guidora) so that their copyright can be acknowledged and/or the material removed from the publication.

Creative Commons Content

We are most grateful to publishers of CreativeCommons material, including images. Our policies concerning this material are (1) to credit the copyright owner, and provide a link where possible (2) to remove Creative Commons material, at once, if the copyright owner so requests - for example, if the owner changes the licensing of an image.

We will also keep our interpretation of the Creative Commons Non-Commercial license under review. Along with, we believe, most web publishers, our current view is that acceptance of the 'Non-Commercial' condition means (1) we must not sell the image or any publication containing the image (2) we may, however, use an image as an illustration for some information which is not being sold or offered for sale.

Note to other copyright owners

We are grateful to those copyright owners who have given permission for their material to be used. Some of the material comes from secondary and tertiary sources. In every case, we have tried to locate the original author or photographer and make the appropriate acknowledgment. In some cases, the sources have proved obscure, and we have been unable to track them down. In these cases, we would like to hear from the copyright owners and will be pleased to acknowledge them in future editions or remove the material.

Made in United States
Troutdale, OR
10/15/2023

13755654R00073